Constructing a Collective Memory of the Holocaust

Aldham Robarts LRC

Liverpool John Moores University

**Books are to be returned on or before
the last date below.**

2 3 MAY 1997

2 3 JAN 2004

LIBREX—

LIVERPOOL JMU LIBRARY

3 1111 00599 4726

CONSTRUCTING A COLLECTIVE
MEMORY OF THE HOLOCAUST

꙰

A Life History of Two Brothers' Survival

RONALD J. BERGER

LIVERPOOL
JOHN MOORES UNIVERSITY
TRUEMAN STREET LIBRARY
TEL. 051 231 4022/4023

UNIVERSITY PRESS OF COLORADO

© 1995 by the University Press of Colorado

Published by the University Press of Colorado
P.O. Box 849
Niwot, Colorado 80544

All rights reserved.
Printed in the United States of America.

The University Press of Colorado is a cooperative publishing enterprise supported, in part, by Adams State College, Colorado State University, Fort Lewis College, Mesa State College, Metropolitan State College of Denver, University of Colorado, University of Northern Colorado, University of Southern Colorado, and Western State College of Colorado.

Portions of this book originally appeared in "Agency, Structure, and Jewish Survival of the Holocaust: A Life History Study," *The Sociological Quarterly*, vol. 36, no. 1, © 1995 The Midwest Sociological Society. Reprinted with permission.

The paper used in this publication meets the minimum requirements of the American National Standard for Information Sciences — Permanence of Paper for Printed Library Materials. ANSI Z39.48-1984

Library of Congress Cataloging-in-Publication Data

Berger, Ronald J.
    Constructing a collective memory of the Holocaust: a life history of two brothers' survival / Ronald J. Berger.
        p.   cm.
    Includes bibliographical references and index.
    ISBN: 0-87081-368-4 (alk. paper)
    1. Jews — Poland — Biography. 2. Holocaust, Jewish (1939–1945) — Underground movements, Jewish — Poland. I. Title.
DS135.P63A125 1995
940.53'18'0922438 — dc20   95-159
                                                      CIP

10 9 8 7 6 5 4 3 2 1

For the third generation,
Sarah, Jesse, Daniel, Alex, and Tara

In memory of my beloved father,
Michael Berger, 1921–1994

Contents

Preface

A Second-Generation Perspective

I was exposed to very little about the Holocaust growing up in the 1950s and 1960s, even though my father was a survivor of the Nazi's genocidal campaign against the Jews of Europe. I knew that my father had been in a concentration camp during World War II, but as far as I could tell, the only observable trace of that experience was the blue tattooed number on his arm. Recently my father reminded me that when I was six or seven years old, I had asked him why I only had grandparents on my mother's side of the family while all of my friends had two sets of grandparents. At that time all that he told me was that they had died. When I was a little older, he did tell me about his being in a concentration camp and about his agony over losing his parents. Yet my most vivid images of World War II came from movies about the experiences and heroics of American soldiers. Moreover, I can recall little, if any, attention given to the Holocaust during my years in public school. To be sure, I knew that a large portion of my family had perished during the Nazi years, and I particularly wondered what it would have been like to have known my paternal grandparents. But I did have my maternal grandparents and sufficient numbers of relatives who had emigrated to the United States before the war to maintain a reasonably large extended family.

I was raised in a Jewish enclave on the west side of Los Angeles, an area that my father and American-born mother hoped would insulate my brother and me from anti-Semitism. The public schools I attended had large Jewish populations, and it was not uncommon for classrooms to be virtually empty on the Jewish holidays of Rosh Hashanah and Yom Kippur. At Christmastime I did not feel envious of

Christian children, for my parents were successful in making Hanukkah quite attractive compared to Christmas. As a child I thought that the practice of receiving gifts over an eight-day period was much better than a one-day holiday. Only later did I discover that many Christian children enjoyed a veritable orgy of gifts on that one day, which far surpassed what we may have received during the week-long celebration of Hanukkah.

My parents' religious beliefs can be best described as agnostic, although they hold very strong nationalist sentiments toward Israel and are most definitely culturally identified Jews. During my childhood we observed all the major Jewish holidays. It was assumed that I would be bar mitzvahed, which I was, but further Jewish education was not obligatory. Because I had been raised in a liberal Jewish social milieu, I felt like an assimilated American. I did not feel that being Jewish made me an "outsider" until I moved to southeastern Wisconsin in 1981 when I accepted a teaching position at the University of Wisconsin–Whitewater.

UW–W is located in a small college town between Madison and Milwaukee, about two hours by car from Chicago. In Whitewater and in the neighboring small towns in which I lived for several years, there are few, if any, Jews. Within a month or two after I first arrived, I was invited to dinner at a faculty member's house. The conversation turned to religion when our hostess asserted, in what seemed like a non sequitur, "Those Jews have a lot of nerve thinking they are the 'chosen people!'" When I told her that I was Jewish, she was embarrassed and apologized. Later I found out that this woman had been educated in Catholic parochial schools. But what stuck in my mind was how ingrained contemporary anti-Semitism must be. At other times I heard expressions pertaining to people who would "Jew you down," and once when I was in a grocery store, someone told me an anti-Semitic joke, not knowing I would find it offensive. I felt invisible. Even a little seven-year-old girl who was a neighbor of mine expressed confusion to her parents when she found out I was Jewish because she thought that all "Jews had horns."

At the time I was unaware of a growing collective consciousness among the second generation of children of Holocaust survivors. Eva Fogelman, one of the first to write about the second generation, traces this movement in large part to the more general cultural interest in "roots" that emerged in the United States in the 1970s and to the increased visibility of anti-Semitism in Europe in the 1980s.[1] Members of the second generation have been making important contributions to scholarly research on the Holocaust and to the education of the post-Holocaust generations. Importantly, they have also been helping survivors explore their memories and provide testimonies of their experiences. Maria Rosenbloom notes that this cross-generational mutual rediscovery of the past has been a bonding experience for the first and second generations and has symbolically substituted for "the rituals of mourning" and the absence of "graves, headstones and burial places which were so cruelly denied to the victims" and their families.[2]

My interest in exploring my father's past was piqued at a lecture I attended at my university in the latter part of 1987. Robert Clary, the actor who is most known for his role as Louis LaBeau in the television sitcom Hogan's Heroes, spoke to a standing-room-only audience of about eight hundred people. I had never seen so many people turn out for an event at the university. Clary explained that for most of his life he had kept quiet about the Holocaust because he had not wanted to "rehash" his "thirty-one months of hell." But as he turned sixty, he explained, he began to realize that it would not be long until there were no longer any survivors alive to tell their story. He was particularly concerned about the so-called Holocaust revisionists, including those with scholarly credentials, who continue to deny that the atrocities occurred.[3]

During the audience question-and-answer period, I was taken aback by a woman who identified herself as twenty-five years old and who said she was outraged that she had "never heard of the Holocaust." However, what also struck me was how little I actually knew about the Holocaust and about what had happened to my father and his family. Through my previous work as a sociologist, I had been concerned with questions of class, race, and gender. It now occurred to me how much I had failed to inquire into my own Jewish heritage, as if it contained nothing of value beyond mere personal concerns. Thus, I became interested in making a contribution toward preserving the memory of the Holocaust — and my father's experience in particular — in the context of my work as a sociologist. I began talking with my father about the Holocaust, and we decided to tape-record his account. He was pleased that I was interested in his experience and that he was going to be able to leave "a legacy for my family." He also suggested that I talk to his brother, my uncle, as well.

When I first suggested to my father and uncle that I wanted to turn their narratives into a book, they were a little apprehensive. Had not similar stories been told many times before? Did they have anything to say that would be of interest to persons outside of the family? I replied that I thought they had a story that was worth telling and that it was important to give a voice to survivors like themselves who had not had the opportunity to speak about the Holocaust for so many years. I also hoped that I might be able to add a sociological perspective to their personal accounts that would lend some insight into the phenomenon of survival.

To be sure, I approached this task with some trepidation. Were there not Jews who felt that the Holocaust was "a sacred and essentially incomprehensible event" that was beyond description, especially through social science?[4] I found myself, like Gerald Markle and associates, writing about survivors with some discomfort, fearing unintentional "trivialization and disrespect."[5] Yet I was encouraged by those historical scholars who argue against mystifying the Holocaust as beyond intellectual discourse.[6] Shamai Davidson, who has worked extensively with Holocaust survivors, suggests that the accumulation of many oral histories may make possible a perspective on Holocaust survival that was even "denied some individual survivors as they were preoccupied by the bitter drama of their own [struggle]."[7]

During the course of researching my father and uncle's life histories, I benefited from a Faculty Development Grant from the University of Wisconsin System that gave me the time to immerse myself in the scholarly literature and to prepare to teach a course on the Holocaust. I was also aided by a UW–Whitewater sabbatical that allowed me time to complete this book. Parts of the book were developed for an article that appeared in *The Sociological Quarterly*. I wish to thank Norman Denzin, editor of TSQ, and the reviewers of that journal for their helpful comments and suggestions on that article. Thanks go as well to Luther Wilson, Laurie Sirotkin, and Jody Berman of the University Press of Colorado for their support of this project, and to Jess Dev

Lionheart for her excellent work as copy editor. I also thank my wife, Ruthy, for her patience during the hours I was working on the manuscript and for her valuable editorial assistance. Finally, I am deeply appreciative of my father, Michael Berger, and my uncle, Shlomo Berger, for their willingness to relive the horror they experienced and to tell their stories.

Constructing a Collective Memory of the Holocaust

CHAPTER 1

Collective Memory and Jewish Holocaust Survival

The concept of collective memory was originally advanced by Maurice Halbachs to describe recollections of "a shared past that are retained by members of a group . . . that experienced it."[1] Barry Schwartz views the term as a metaphor for a "society's retention and loss of information about its past" but notes that only part of this memory is defined by individuals who actually lived through the events, what Halbachs calls "autobiographical memory."[2] In the case of the Nazi Holocaust against the Jews, the second-generation "children of survivors" have acquired a special sensitivity to the Holocaust that others of their generation do not have.[3] They have felt a responsibility to share their awareness with others and to help their elders explore their memories and provide testimonies of their experiences during the war years.

This book represents such a cross-generational construction of a collective memory of the Holocaust. It is a life history study that combines personal narrative and sociological analysis to provide an interpretive account of two Polish Jewish brothers who survived the Holocaust: Michael Berger, who is my father, was incarcerated in several concentration camps, including the Auschwitz camps at Birkenau and Buna-Monowitz; and Shlomo Berger, who is my uncle, escaped the camps passing as a Christian Pole with a construction crew, the Polish Partisans, and the Soviet Army.

Life history research in sociology peaked in the 1930s but declined as social science moved in a more quantitative direction. In recent years, however, there has been renewed interest in the life history method as a means of advancing sociological theory and of understanding history through ordinary people's experiences. The life history is a form of sociological discourse that respects "human subjects as individuals who can tell true stories about their lives."[4] In the case of Jewish survivors of the Nazi period, it is also a means of bearing witness or providing "testimonial proof" of the events and experiences that have come to be known as the Holocaust.[5]

Compared to other scholarly disciplines, sociology has had relatively little to say about the Holocaust. Yet Zygmunt Bauman argues that this watershed historical event affords opportunities to examine issues that are central to some of the "main themes of sociological inquiry."[6] In this book I utilize the life history of two brothers' survival to explore one of the central problems of general social theory: the relationship between human agency and social structure.[7] I did not assume or identify a priori this focus on agency and structure; it emerged in the course of the research.[8] I appropriate "agency" and "structure" as fundamental presuppositional categories of generalized sociological discourse.[9] As such, they provide a foundation for developing a distinctly sociological alternative to the psychological theorizing that has dominated the survivor literature and to characterizations of Jews that have been overly negative or overly heroic.

C. Wright Mills argues that "no social study that does not come back to the problems of biography, of history and of their intersections within a society has completed its intellectual journey."[10] However, current expositions of a general theory of agency and structure focus on the development of abstract conceptual schemes.[11] I do not attempt to advance this theory per se but to ground it in "the world of problematic lived experience."[12] In this regard I share interactionist sociologists' interest in providing descriptive interpretations of ordinary individuals interacting in particular historical moments. Although genocides are nonroutine, they are recurrent social phenomena. Analyses of survivors' experiences can help inform us about how individuals survive such ruptures in everyday life and, more generally, how people respond to and overcome adversity.

According to Robert Lifton, a "survivor" is someone who remains alive after encountering, being exposed to, or witnessing death.[13] Holocaust survivors lived through a persistent "condition of extremity" that appeared beyond their "ability to alter or end" and that illustrated "what it meant (and means) in our time to exist with-out a sense of human agency."[14]

Agency involves the capacity to exert control and to some extent even transform "the social relations in which one is enmeshed."[15] However, most Holocaust survivors attribute their staying alive primarily to chance, luck, or miracles.[16] As Terrence Des Pres observes, "The moments of salvation [were] so unexpected, that the power of human encounters seemed slight and difficult to make sense of."[17] But even though survivors often felt unable "to influence their destiny," they also recount making choices and taking purposeful actions on those occasions when opportunities were available.[18]

Holocaust survivors' accounts are permeated with what Norman Denzin describes as "epiphanies," that is, interactional moments of crisis that leave indelible "marks on people's lives" and through which "personal character is manifested."[19] Holocaust epiphanies often include "crucial moments" in which difficult choices and quick decisions that were the difference between life and death were made.[20] In Jean-Paul Sartre's terms, epiphanies contain a "coefficient of adversity" where external conditions put up "actual resistance" to agency.[21] As such, Holocaust epiphanies illuminate the relationship between agency and structure in instances where the tension between them is heightened and the individual resides in a "no-man's-land betwixt and between . . . the past and the . . . future."[22]

JEWISH PARTICULARITY, SILENCE, AND EMOTIONAL REMINDERS

According to Halbachs, collective memories are social reconstructions of the past that reflect the concerns and interests of different groups and that adapt "the image of ancient facts to the beliefs and spiritual needs of the present."[23] Most non–Jewish Americans' memory of World War II in Europe focuses on the role of the U. S. armed forces in thwarting Adolf Hitler's attempt to achieve world domination.[24] In contrast, most Jews remember the war foremost for the Nazis' "final solution," which resulted in the death of 60 percent of European Jewry, approximately one-third of the world's Jewish population.[25] At the Nuremberg trials following the war, the particu-

larity of Jewish victimization during the Nazi period was acknowledged but subsumed under the broader category of "crimes against
humanity" and was soon "half forgotten."[26] Similarly, early works
written by Jewish victims and survivors — such as Anne Frank's
diary, Elie Wiesel's *Night*, and Primo Levi's *If This Be a Man* — were first
printed in limited editions and were largely ignored.[27]

In the first decade after the war the suppression of memory of
the Jewish experience was also apparent in the relationships survivors had with those outside of the survivor community. This silence
was in part a function of guilt for having lived when others had not
and of "shame [for] telling a story that must [have appeared] unbelievable and . . . entirely out of tune with surrounding society."[28]
Survivors who wanted to forget their trauma were also encouraged
to do so by others around them who wanted to put the war in the
past and move on with their lives. Among Jews "the realization that
'this could have happened to me'" led potential listeners to close
their ears.[29] Survivors who insisted on talking about their experiences were often perceived as psychologically deficient and in need
of treatment.[30] Israeli Jews in particular — who envisioned a society
of self-reliant "new men" achieving mastery over their environment
by returning to the land and fighting for independence — at times
held rather disdainful attitudes toward survivors. According to Shamai Davidson, for a long time many Israelis implicitly urged Holocaust survivors "to forget their past . . . and to emerge from their
background of powerlessness, helplessness, and defenselessness into
a new Israeli identity" that repudiated what Israelis perceived as the
passivity of the European Jews during the Holocaust.[31] Thus, Israelis
lent a more receptive ear toward those survivors who had fought as
partisans or who had been involved in armed resistance during the
war. In fact, Israelis sought after these individuals, treated them as
heroes, and urged them to relate their experiences.

Nevertheless, the 1961 trial of Adolf Eichmann marked a turning
point in the postwar memory of the Holocaust. In the minds of
Israeli officials, the purpose of the trial was not merely to punish
Eichmann but to impress on the other nations of the world their
moral obligation to support the Jewish state.[32] During the trial, testimonies from scores of witnesses were heard, though even here the
more heroic modes of survivor resistance were emphasized.[33]

The Eichmann trial was, in Raymond Schmitt's terms, an "emotional reminder," an event or experience that called forth "memories and feelings that ha[d] been retained in the psychic body."[34] It was the first time that the particularity of Jewish victimization was brought into focus worldwide and the first time that large numbers of survivors began telling their stories in public. Several years later the 1967 Six-Day War between Israel and its Arab neighbors renewed fears among Jews that a second Holocaust was possible. However, the decisive Israeli victory in that conflict brought pride and confidence to Jews around the world and legitimized Israel as a capable ally of the United States, "worthy of support on pragmatic as well as moral grounds."[35] Building on the financial security that Jews had achieved in the United States, survivors increasingly felt empowered to become more vocal about their wartime experiences. By the late 1970s the Holocaust had begun receiving widespread exposure in print and film, especially through the 1978 airing of the television docudrama Holocaust, based on the Gerald Green screenplay.[36] Gradually survivors who had been "deprived for so many years of respectful listeners to their stories" came to see themselves as responsible for reminding the world that what happened to them must happen "Never Again!"[37] With survivors approaching the last years of their lives, they have become concerned that when they are gone, no one will be left to discredit those who deny the Holocaust. Elie Wiesel's worst nightmare is that "I wake up shivering, thinking that when we die, no one will be able to persuade people that the Holocaust occurred."[38]

SCHOLARLY CHARACTERIZATIONS OF HOLOCAUST SURVIVAL

In my view the most pressing question is not whether the Holocaust will be remembered but how it will be remembered. Much of the initial scholarly research on Jewish victims and survivors characterized their responses in largely negative terms. Jews were viewed as passively accepting their fate, as going "like sheep to the slaughter."[39] The Jewish Councils organized by the Nazis to carry out their edicts were criticized for being overly compliant and for collaborating with the Nazis. In one of the most influential appraisals of concentration camp behavior, Bruno Bettelheim suggested that inmates typically regressed to a childish dependency on the SS guards, experienced deindividuation, abandoned previously inculcated norms and values, and eventually identified completely with their oppressors.[40] Others characterized Jewish behavior in the camps as fatalistic, self-destructive, divisive, corrupt, and predatory.[41] Survivors after the war were described as guilt-ridden, emotionally withdrawn, "chronically depressed, anxious, and fearful."[42]

Des Pres was one of the first to observe that these formulations were derived from limited observations and were misleading as generalizations.[43] For instance, Bettelheim developed his thesis on the basis of camp conditions in the 1930s at a time when prisoners who held positions of power (trustees) were not political prisoners or Jews but those who had been convicted of predatory crimes of theft and violence, including murder. Analysts have increasingly adopted a more nuanced view of the variety and complexity of human response to extremity and have turned their attention to the constructive strategies for survival that emerged during the Nazi period. Individuals who survived conditions of extremity often emerged from an initial period of shock, despair, and disbelief able to realistically appraise their situation and take strategic courses of action through calculated risk-taking and disobedience. Moreover, many were able to do so without completely abandoning prewar norms of human reciprocity and systems of morality. For example, Des Pres notes that survivors' accounts emphasize the "all against all" atmosphere but also regularly include reports of people holding onto their humanity and offering each other "help and mutual care." Anna Pawełczyńska argues that individuals "who made no revisions" in pre-existing humanitarian values perished if they "applied them in an absolute way" but that there were always those who united "together in the practice of the basic norm, 'Do not harm your neighbor and, if possible, save him.'" Mary Gallant and Jay Cross characterize survivors as individuals who acquired a "challenged identity" that gave them the will to go on by observing others' courageous responses to this common ordeal. Davidson describes the group bonding in the camps, which provided individuals with mutual aid and helped them maintain hope and preserve "a sense of self despite the dehumanization and amorality."[44]

As I suggested earlier, scholarly interpretations of human agency during the Holocaust often psychologize survival and view it as a matter endogenous to individuals rather than as a social process. For instance, Des Pres emphasizes survivors' inherent will to live, which he describes as an evolutionary pattern or "biological imperative." Viktor Frankl argues that survivors' adjustments to camp life "show that man does have a choice of action" but that this choice results more from an "inner decision" than from external circumstances. Michael Unger highlights the role of internal defense mechanisms, which enabled individuals to block out the horror and focus on their survival needs. Gerhard Botz describes survivors in terms of their capacity for voluntaristic conduct, outward adaptation to the environment, sociability, and readiness to offer and receive support from others. William Helmreich attributes individuals' ability to stay alive to "personality traits" or inner qualities such as assertiveness, tenacity, courage, willingness to take risks, flexibility, optimism, and intelligence. He concludes that the "story of the survivors is one of courage and strength, of people who are living proof of the indomitable will of human beings to survive and of their tremendous capacity for hope, . . . a story of just how remarkable people can be."[45]

Lawrence Langer, however, cautions against turning survivors' personal tragedy into "triumphant accounts" where even "passivity" and dying with "dignity" are romanticized as forms of "resistance."[46] According to Langer, surviving the Holocaust "was a thoroughly practical matter" that had little to do with "a victory of the human spirit." The challenge for the analyst is to enter the survivors' world and "find an orientation that will do justice to their recaptured experience *without* summoning it or them to judgment and evaluation."[47]

Among current analyses, Patricia Benner, Ethel Roskies, and Richard Lazarus most closely approximate a social theory of agency and structure through a general model of stress and coping behavior. They characterize stress as a relational concept that reflects "reciprocity between external demands, constraints, and resources" and "internal resources to manage them." They do not view survivors as helpless victims or passive responders to circumstances but as persons who attempted to manipulate the stress experience to achieve some degree of control over "those small segments of reality that could be managed . . . [and contained] possibilities for direct action." Coping proceeded through cognitive appraisal of the stress situation and evaluation of available resources and options. Actions were then taken on the basis of this appraisal. "Any cessation of appraisal, as in the case of individuals who withdrew into . . . [a] state of apathy, . . . was a signal of impending death."[48]

Although an advance over previous formulations, Benner, Roskies, and Lazarus fall short of offering a distinctly sociological framework for analyzing survivors' experiences. Their stress-coping model can be recast in terms of a more general social theory of agency and structure in ways that can advance understanding of Jewish Holocaust survival and that can help inform us about how individuals respond to and overcome adversity.

Human Agency and Social Structure: A Framework for Analyzing Holocaust Survival

In this life history study I adopt concepts from Anthony Giddens's and William Sewell's work on agency and structure to provide an interpretive framework for examining the two brothers' survival experiences.[49] In doing so, I make no commitment to their theories in toto. Rather, I appropriate their theories to construct a general "sensitizing scheme" that allows me to enhance my analysis with concepts derived from interactionist sociologists who work outside of the agency-structure tradition.[50]

In a reformulation of Giddens's concepts, Sewell views social structure as consisting of *cultural schemas* and *resources*. Cultural schemas refer to generalized prescriptions for action, both formal and informal, including modes of thought, conventions, habits of speech, and gestures. Resources refer to capabilities, both human and nonhuman, that enable actors to acquire, maintain, or generate power in social interactions.

Agency, as suggested earlier, involves the capacity to exert control and to some extent even transform socially imposed relationships. It entails "an ability to coordinate one's actions with others and against others . . . and to monitor the simultaneous effects of one's own and others' activities."[51] This conception is consistent with interactionists' view of individuals as capable of "'minded,' self-reflexive behavior" and of "shaping and guiding" their own and others' actions.[52]

Gallant and Cross offer a symbolic interactionist interpretation of Holocaust survivors' responses that focuses on the subjective processes by which individuals in the Nazi concentration camps reconstructed a "challenged identity" from their initially disorienting and depersonifying experience. This identity involved a strengthened "resolve to endure and in some way change . . . conditions, . . . if only by actively transforming the meaning of events." Gallant and Cross argue that there was "no particular socialization . . . that would specifically prepare someone" for the survival experience other than "general socialization processes . . . [that] prepared the individual to assert the autonomy of the self."[53] My theory of agency and structure differs from this analysis in three respects: (1) it is not restricted to concentration camp life but covers the experience of Jews passing outside the camps; (2) the transformation of events was more than symbolic, for it involved the acquisition of material resources, such as food and physical protection from the weather and human antagonists, that made living possible; and (3) there were prewar structural influences that helped individuals accomplish this transformation.

Structural-oriented sociologists have criticized some interactionists for underestimating the extent to which "action is organized by structural constraints that are, in some sense, external to any particular actor."[54] However, Sewell argues that structures are both constraining and enabling. Individuals "are born with only a highly generalized capacity for agency, analogous to their ability to use language. . . . Agency is formed by a specific range of cultural schemas and resources available in a person's social milieu" and entails individuals' ability to apply or extend "their structurally formed capacities" to new circumstances in "creative and innovative ways."[55]

In the case of the Holocaust the social structure of the Nazi regime was systematically organized to accomplish the persecution and eventual elimination of all Jews.[56] But as the following life history indicates, some Jews' ability to exercise agency to stay alive under these structural conditions of extremity was influenced by their prewar exposure to cultural schemas and resources that they were able to transpose to the war-occupation context. As the eminent Holocaust historian Raul Hilberg argues, "Survival was not altogether random. . . . Although the German destruction process was a massive leveler, it did not obliterate" all prewar differences. However, he adds, these differences acquired new meaning during the Nazi period. They were no longer a measure of high or low status but an indicator of more or less vulnerability. For example, age was a key resource, for survivors were more likely to be relatively young (between their teens and thirties) and of "good health at the start of the ordeal."[57] These physical resources maximized their ability to endure hardship and withstand disease. In addition, Jews with particular occupational skills — such as carpenters, tailors, shoemakers, and physicians — also fared better, for they remained useful to others who might want to keep them alive.

At the same time, Jews' ability to exercise agency successfully during the Holocaust was in large part an interpersonal accomplishment that was "laden with collectively produced differences in power."[58] In the concentration camps, for instance, survival required an ability to "organize," to use the camp lexicon, that is, to acquire life-sustaining resources through unauthorized means. Successful organization was a matter of collective action and derived from a person's position in the functional hierarchy of the camp and the network of social relationships among inmates.[59] Similarly, Jews who survived outside the camps by passing as Christians were generally dependent on the support they received from members of the non-Jewish population.[60]

It would be unwise, however, to overestimate individuals' ability to overcome conditions of extremity and assign privileged status to agency over structure in social analyses. During the Holocaust all that individuals could hope to accomplish was to hold on a little longer until external conditions over which they had no control changed, that is, until the Allies defeated the Germans in a military confrontation. Moreover, as Giddens reminds us, agency must be distinguished from intentions.[61] Human interaction always contains "an emergent, negotiated, often unpredictable" quality, and thus the consequences of actions may differ from those that are intended.[62] As Sartre would have it, "My field of action is perpetually traversed by the appearances and disappearances of objects with which I have nothing to do. . . . Every free project . . . anticipates a margin of unpredictability due to the independence of things . . . [and] a thousand foreseeable and unforeseeable accidents . . . [that] constitute its meaning."[63]

METHODOLOGY: CONSTRUCTING A LIFE HISTORY STUDY

This life history study focuses on the experiences of two Holocaust survivors from the Polish town of Krosno: Michael and Shlomo Berger. In the research I adopted what Ingeborg Helling describes as a "narrative interview" approach. In the first stage I asked the brothers to reconstruct their experiences as best as they could recollect "according to [their] own relevancies."[64] As is common with autobiographical memories in general and Holocaust accounts in particular, Michael and Shlomo found a chronological organization of their experience to be the most effective means of retrieving memory.[65] In addition, as Denzin notes, life histories often rely on "conventionalized, narrative expressions . . . which structure how lives are told and written about."[66] Michael and Shlomo implicitly relied on such conventions and constructed a narrative with a beginning and an end, objective markers, turning points, and epiphanies.

In the early part of 1988 Michael began tape-recording his narrative alone in the privacy of his home. I transcribed the recording and gave Shlomo the opportunity to read it. Afterward he recorded a narrative of his own that expanded on Michael's account of experiences they held in common and that described the particulars of his situation. In the next stage I tape-recorded (separate) open-ended interviews with the brothers and prompted them to further develop their narratives and fill in gaps in their reconstruction of the events. I made every effort not to take the initiative away from them.

Michael and Shlomo's recall ability was rather impressive in spite of the time that had elapsed. The Holocaust was a "major epiphany" for Jewish survivors, a life-shattering event that contained elements of uniqueness, consequentiality, unexpectedness, and emotionality that facilitate memory retrieval.[67] As Langer observes, there is often "no need to revive what has never died. . . . Though slumbering memories may crave reawakening, . . . Holocaust memory is an insomniac faculty, whose mental eyes have never slept."[68] Like other Holocaust survivors, the brothers' memories have also been kept alive by the emotional reminders of the postwar period, including contemporary news events such as President Ronald Reagan's 1985 visit to Bitburg.[69] In addition, Michael has the constant reminder of the concentration camp tattoo number on his arm. Importantly, participating in the research itself was an emotional reminder that helped stimulate the brothers' memories, although this involved some painful reliving of the events. However, there were so many layers of experience to unfold, and as both Michael and Shlomo remarked, "every day was a story in itself."

In the course of the research I attempted to mitigate potential problems of internal validity. In Michael's case I could evaluate elements of his Auschwitz account by referring to writings of other Auschwitz survivors.[70] In Shlomo's case I was able to interview a Pole from Krosno, Tadeusz Duchowski, who had helped him pass while on location working with a Polish construction crew during the war. Duchowski corroborated Shlomo's account and contributed details to this episode that Shlomo had forgotten. I also interviewed Duchowski's wife, who had helped Shlomo make contact with her husband. She corroborated the general features of the brothers' account of the Nazi occupation of Krosno and the liquidation of the Jewish community in that town.[71] In addition, I consulted other published sources that are relevant to their experiences.[72]

At the same time, there is no reason to assume that other accounts written at the time (for example, diaries or letters) more accurately represent what transpired than those remembered years later. Although the former representations are often perceived as more authoritative than those "shaped through hindsight, . . . [they] may be less reliable in a 'factual sense' because of their proximity to the events."[73] They may have been written to elicit particular responses to what was occurring (for example, to move allies or potential victims to action) or to disguise information (for example, regarding resistance efforts) that the writer feared might fall into the wrong hands. In any case Geoffrey Hartman suggests that we "not try to turn the survivor into a historian, but to value him [or her] as a witness to a dehumanizing situation."[74]

External validity is another potential concern in life history research. Michael and Shlomo do not have the literary skills, professional training (for example, psychiatry), or religious commitments of authors of some of the most well-known survivor accounts.[75] Nor were they among the more elite members of the camps or those who were privy to the inner workings of resistance efforts. Nevertheless, their very survival indicates that they were not individuals who were entirely overwhelmed by the unfolding of the events. They represent ordinary Jews who are, in Herbert Blumer's terms, well-informed observers who have expertise because they experienced the Holocaust.[76] They are extraordinary only in the sense that they are among the 10 percent of Polish Jewry who did manage to survive the war.[77]

Denzin cautions that the "reactive effects of the observer" need to be monitored in life history research.[78] The potential for bias may be of concern in this case because the subjects are relatives. This problem is often present in life history research, where it is not unusual for subjects and observers to become close friends. However, I do not believe that either Michael or Shlomo would have been willing to focus in as much detail on their experiences if the interview had been conducted by an "outsider." Although I felt able to maintain the role of the professional interviewer, I took seriously Nora Levin's concern that Holocaust survivors not be forced to suffer their experiences "once literally and then imaginatively again."[79] I was thus cautious when probing the brothers in ways that elicited this emotional pain of memory. Michael feels that the experience "hardened" him and says that he gets "choked up" only when he thinks about the loss of his family. Shlomo notes that "it was an experience that there is nothing like. It stays with you for the rest of your life. Twenty years ago I couldn't talk about it without crying. But now I can deal with it." I felt it important to respect the "protective shield" that had helped the brothers restore themselves to the normality of prewar and postwar routines and not push them too far to relive their anguish for the purpose of a more nuanced analysis of the subjective experience of trauma.[80] Michael and Shlomo, like many other survivors, reconstructed their experiences "from the context of normality now" and at times had difficulty finding the words to articulate "the nature of the abnormality then."[81] But this makes their account no less authentic "because how . . . [they] grasped and related

LIVERPOOL JOHN MOORES UNIVERSITY
LEARNING SERVICES

their experiences comprises the actual core of 'their story.'"[82] In spite
of their suffering and deep (though often repressed) sense of family
loss, the brothers are able to think rationally about what transpired
(though at times with anger) and have assimilated their experiences
in a way that has allowed them to move forward with their lives.[83]

As I listened to Michael and Shlomo's stories, I had the feeling
that witness to the Holocaust was being made before my eyes and
that the opportunity to record such testimonies would soon be lost. I
became convinced that there is no substitute for survivors' own
memories. As Judith Miller notes, no one else can speak for them or
"tell us what they have to say."[84] Moreover, I believe that participating in the life history study was a positive experience for both
Michael and Shlomo. They were pleased that they now had the
opportunity to tell their stories and that there would be a permanent
record of their ordeal.[85] Michael indicated that recounting his story
was a welcomed "outlet" that helped him "relieve the burden of my
memory." He said that when he first settled in the United States after
the war, he and other survivors were asked by others (mostly Jews,
including relatives) about their wartime experiences. But "after hearing a little bit about it, they didn't want to hear anymore. Or they
would tell you that 'we suffered, too. Did you know that we couldn't
get any sugar [during the war] and that gasoline was rationed?' It
was as if they were comparing their suffering with ours. Perhaps they
felt guilty about what happened to their European relatives — that
they either didn't do enough to help them or didn't dare to protest
strongly. So we actually stopped talking about it. We felt that nobody
understood us or wanted to understand us."[86]

During the course of this project I accumulated about twenty
hours of narrative-interview material. The "principle of chronol-
ogy," which corresponds to the structure of the brothers' narrative,
provided a logical method of organizing the data for the purpose of
sociological analysis.[87] Chapter 2 begins the life history by briefly sit-
uating Michael and Shlomo's family beginnings in the context of the
history of Jewish-Polish relations. It then considers the influence of
prewar structural conditions on the two brothers' subsequent survival and describes what happened to them at the beginning of
World War II. Chapter 3 provides an account of life under German
occupation in Krosno, the events leading up to the first major liqui-

LIVERPOOL JOHN MOORES UNIVERSITY
LEARNING SERVICES

dation of the Jewish community there, and Michael's eventual deportation. Chapter 4 describes Shlomo's escape and his experiences passing as a non-Jewish Pole with a Polish construction crew, with the Polish Partisans, and with the Soviet Army. Chapter 5 covers the period in which Michael was interned in an SS military camp at Moderówka, in a concentration camp at Szebnie, and in the Auschwitz camps at Birkenau and Buna-Monowitz. Chapter 6 provides an account of Michael's evacuation from Auschwitz and the ordeal of the Death March, as well as his liberation and immediate post-liberation experiences. It also describes what happened to Shlomo after he took leave from the Soviet Army, including his efforts helping Jews emigrate to Palestine and his own difficulties trying to get there. Chapter 7 concludes the book with a review of the life history in light of the agency-structure theme and some observations on memories of suffering and implications for contemporary victimization politics and trends in postmodern social thought.

I did some minor editing of the transcripts for grammar and clarity in order to maintain the focus on the content of Michael and Shlomo's experience rather than on the style of their expression.[88] However, I made every effort to remain faithful to the original accounts and had the brothers examine the final written product. For the most part I present the material in Michael and Shlomo's own words in order to preserve the "testimonial" nature of their accounts, although the book is written as an "edited life history" insofar as I intersperse sociological description and analysis and make reference to other scholarly work.[89] Finally, I wish to reiterate that the agency-structure theme emerged during, rather than preceding, the course of the research.

CHAPTER 2

The Prewar Setting and Early War Years

Poland had the highest concentration of Jews among all European countries prior to World War II, and Polish Jews constituted over half of all the Jews who perished during the Nazis' genocidal campaign.[1] A Jewish presence in Poland can be traced to the tenth century when Jews, often fleeing persecution, emigrated from Germany and Bohemia to the west, from the Byzantine Empire to the south, and from the region east of Romania.[2] In the thirteenth and fourteenth centuries German Jews introduced into Poland the dialect that was to become Yiddish.

Polish princes in various localities granted Jews legal charters that gave them the right to practice their religion as well as to engage in commercial trade and moneylending activities, which were especially open to Jews because of the Catholic church's prohibition of usury. However, this hospitable attitude toward Jews brought hostile reactions from the church, which made efforts to segregate, if not prohibit, Jews from living with Christians in towns under its control. As in other European countries, the church resented Jews for their refusal to adopt the Christian faith. It held Jews almost exclusively responsible for Christ's death and accused them of engaging in "blood libel" (that is, murdering Christian children for religious purposes), of desecrating the body of Christ (that is, despoiling the Christian sacraments of bread and wine), of poisoning wells, and of spreading plagues and famines.[3]

The circumstances of Polish Jews varied from one locality to another. They were often barred from occupational guilds and denied opportunities to own land. Mostly they pursued an economic livelihood as merchants, artisans, or professionals. Although some Jews engaged in agriculture, most lived in urban areas. In the fourteenth and fifteenth centuries Jews played a significant role as middlemen in the trade between Poland and other European countries. Because of links with Jewish communities outside of Poland, Jewish merchants at times gained advantage over non-Jewish businessmen. In addition, Jews functioned in administrative capacities as estate managers for wealthy landowners and the nobility. At times these positions involved collecting taxes and supervising the labor of peasant sharecroppers. All this bred resentment among Poles, especially Ukrainian Poles, who saw Jews as their economic competitors and as the source of their misfortune. Along with the hostility engendered by the church, such resentment often broke out in violent pogroms against the Jewish population.

By the latter part of the eighteenth century Poland was divided among three conquering powers: Russia, Prussia, and Austria. Under these regimes Jews gained a measure of equality, provided they were willing to abandon their religious-cultural traditions and distinctiveness as a people and adopt the culture of the dominant society. According to Israel Gutman, the opportunity for assimilation "found a ready response among a limited sector of wealthy and educated Jews . . . [who] played a role in the development of a capitalist economy in Poland, and . . . [who] distinguished themselves in science . . . and the arts, clearing a path for modern culture to penetrate into Jewish society. But [these Jews] were lost to the Jewish people within a generation or two, whereas the Jewish masses remained faithful to their heritage."[4]

By the early part of the twentieth century Jews remained "a non-assimilable community" that stood out from the general Polish population by their dress, habits, names and surnames, and mannerisms.[5] Polish Jews were also among the poorest of all the Jewish communities on the European continent. Nevertheless, leaders of the rising right-wing Polish nationalist movement began advocating a political program that rejected Jewish assimilation and that, on the eve of World War I, embarked on an aggressive anti-Semitic campaign that included economic boycotts of Jewish businesses. At the same time Zionism, the Jewish nationalist movement, also took hold among some Polish Jews.

Poland gained its sovereignty in the aftermath of the war. But this national rebirth was accompanied by much internal political turmoil and anti-Jewish violence. The 1919 Versailles Minority Treaty that was imposed on Poland guaranteed political rights to minorities, including Jews and Ukrainians, who each constituted about 10 percent of the Polish population. But the treaty was perceived by Poles as an "insult to their national honor," and discrimination and violence against Jews, tolerated if not condoned by the government, became a means of defiance.[6]

Poland experienced fourteen separate governments between 1918 and 1925, until Marshal Józef Piłsudski seized power in a military coup in 1926. The Jews actually fared better under Piłsudski's regime, but after his death in 1935 the new government returned to anti-Semitic zealotry. Efforts were made to dislodge Jews from positions of influence and to close down opportunities for aspiring Jewish youths to be admitted to institutions of higher education. Jews continued to be the object of economic boycotts as well as anti-Semitic propaganda and violence. The Polish government even took a cue from its Nazi neighbor in Germany and began to advocate emigration of Jews as a solution to its so-called Jewish problem. In 1937 in a speech to the Polish parliament, Foreign Minister Józef Beck argued that Poland had space for only 0.5 million of the estimated 3.3 million Jews who lived in Poland at that time. Such was the state of affairs for Jews on the eve of World War II.

FAMILY BEGINNINGS AND PREWAR INFLUENCES

Michael and Shlomo Berger grew up against this historical backdrop. They were both born in Krosno, a small town of less than ten thousand people in the western Galacia region of southeastern Poland. Krosno had a viable local economy, with a glass factory, oil refinery, and shoe and rubber factory; and it was known as the place where the first lamp lit with kerosene was invented. Jews had come to Krosno in the fifteenth century and before the war had established a community of about twenty-five hundred with important local

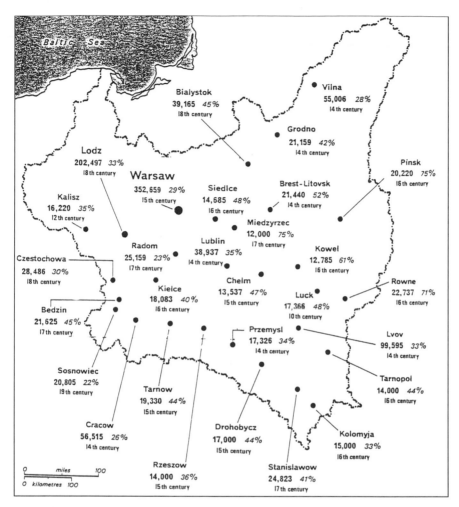

Poland's largest Jewish communities on the eve of World War II. Copyright © by Martin Gilbert, *Atlas of the Holocaust* (2nd ed.), William Morrow, New York, 1993.

institutions that included a loan association, Gemilat Chesed, and a charity organization, Tomchey Aneeyim.[7]

Jacob Berger (1873–1942), Michael and Shlomo's father, was a tailor by trade who had bought a home for cash when he was in his teens. Jacob had two wives. With Miriam Fabian Rieger (1876–1908), his first wife, he had five daughters — Helena (1897–1938), Frances (1900–1985), Bertha (1902–1942), Eleanor (1904–1987),

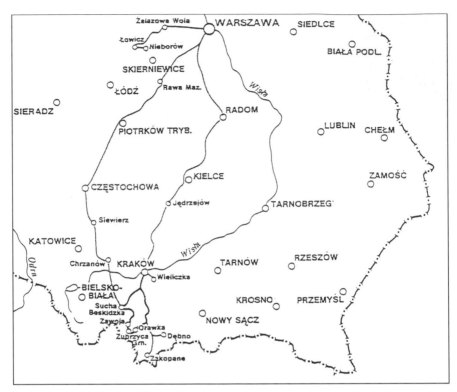

Krosno on postwar Polish map of southeastern Poland.

and Rose (1906–). When Miriam died, Jacob married Miriam's younger sister, Rosa (1893–1942), as was the Jewish custom at that time. Rosa gave birth to four sons — Moishe (1913–1943), Joshua (1916-1943), Shlomo (1919–), and Michael (1921–1994).

Four of the five sisters emigrated from Poland before World War II. Frances and Eleanor went to the United States in 1920, first to Chicago and later to Los Angeles, before Michael was even born. Helena and Rose left for Berlin when Michael and Shlomo were still young children, and just prior to the outbreak of World War II Rose managed to obtain immigration papers to leave Nazi Germany and join her sisters in Los Angeles.[8] The four brothers had applied for U.S. visas and were awaiting approval when the war stopped all emigration. As Michael recalls, "My parents had many occasions to emigrate from Poland, but my father always refused to leave since he was well established and considered Poland his homeland. However, my brothers and I were of a different mind, and we wanted to follow our

older sisters to the United States. We applied for and received affida-
vits [sponsorship papers] from our sisters, who now lived in Los
Angeles. These papers were registered with the American consul in
Warsaw, and according to the consul, we were to receive visas to
enter the U.S. in 1941. Unfortunately, this was not to be."

As I indicated in Chapter 1, some Jews' ability to survive the
Holocaust was influenced by prewar experiences that could later be
transposed to the war-occupation context. Although Jacob and Rosa
Berger remained steadfast about staying in Poland themselves, the
family cultural milieu appears to have been conducive to the development of personal qualities, such as flexibility and a willingness to
take risks, that were important to Michael and Shlomo's subsequent
survival.[9]

More important, however, the training Michael and Shlomo
received in tailoring gave them a resource they were able to exchange
during the war years for favors and essential provisions both inside
and outside the concentration camps. Michael recalls, "My father
believed that each of his sons should have a trade. Thus, after each
one of us completed seven years of public school and two years of
night school, we joined him in his tailor shop. Shlomo and Joshua
were 'master tailors,' which meant they had a license from a trade
guild. . . . I am convinced that the tailoring skills we acquired were
a major reason that Shlomo and I survived the war."

The family tailor shop, which operated out of the Bergers' home,
also provided many occasions for Michael and Shlomo to have contact with the non-Jewish population. Research on helping behavior
during the Holocaust finds that Christian Poles with prior relationships with Jews were more likely than those without such relationships to lend assistance.[10] The Duchowskis, who later helped Shlomo
pass as a Christian, were customers whom Shlomo had known and
with whom he had had pleasant interactions before the war.

Knowledge of non-Jewish cultural schemas, including language
and religion, was also crucial to Jewish survival, particularly outside
of the camps,[11] where, in Erving Goffman's terms, impression man-
agement skills were necessary to maintain a "front" or orchestrate a
"performance" as someone who was not Jewish.[12] In prewar Poland
more than half the Jewish children attended special Jewish schools
that inhibited mastery of the Polish language.[13] But as boys Michael

and Shlomo attended school in mixed classes and played with Christian children. While the Berger family was by no means assimilated, the brothers acquired social skills that enabled them to interact effectively with non-Jews.

This is not to say that the brothers' relationship to the dominant Christian population was always harmonious. Although Michael remembers having many Jewish as well as non-Jewish friends, "our friendship with non-Jewish children was somewhat strained, alternating between being friendly and hostile. There were always fights between the Polish and Jewish kids during recess at school and after school. Yet we played with the very same kids. A [non-Jewish] friend whom I later met in Krosno over forty years after the war reminded me that the Polish kids used to leave me alone because I was rather small and everyone liked me."

Michael recalls with more acrimony the teachers who discriminated against him. "In my school, classes were held from Monday through Saturday. While the Jewish students were excused from attending classes on Shabbes, some of my teachers chose to teach on Saturdays all the new basic steps that a student needed in order to master a given subject. Upon my return to school on Monday, I was bewildered to find myself behind the Polish students. To this day I can't forgive my math teacher for introducing fractions in our absence. He did that on purpose to hold us back and keep us from excelling." Shlomo, too, remembers being disadvantaged by such practices. "The teachers gave special homework assignments on Saturdays, and we had to have our homework turned in on Monday, or we would receive a failing grade. We found out what happened in school from our Polish friends, but we couldn't keep up with them."

Importantly, the brothers did acquire language skills as youths. Shlomo learned a little German in school, which helped the brothers through some encounters with German soldiers at the beginning of the war. Later Shlomo and Michael's facility with Ukrainian, which is similar to Russian, enabled them to negotiate black market transactions with the Soviets to acquire essential provisions. Toward the end of the war Shlomo was able to capitalize on his language skills by assisting a Soviet officer in charge of German prisoners of war.

In prewar Poland Jews who observed religious rules that dictated special rituals and dress often looked and behaved in ways that made them different from non-Jews.[14] During the war this characteristic limited Jews' ability to pass as Christian Poles. This observation should not, however, be misconstrued as suggesting that Jews with strong religious commitments did not survive the war. Indeed, for many Jews such commitments were crucial in helping them endure their suffering.[15] However, Michael and Shlomo's religious views can best be described as agnostic, although the Berger family did keep an orthodox Jewish home and the boys retained a respect for Jewish traditions. Michael notes, "I never identified with the Orthodox view of Judaism, and on a daily basis prayer and ritual meant very little to me." Similarly, Shlomo recalls attending Hebrew school until he was fifteen years old, "but later I just strayed." As boys their parents expected them to follow the Jewish tradition of keeping their heads covered, but they often removed their caps when outside of the home. With the exception of circumcision, there was nothing about their physical appearance that would have prevented them from passing as Poles. In fact, Michael remarks that to this day "I resent Abraham" for the circumcision that marked him as a Jew. For Shlomo, however, it was especially significant that he later learned about Roman Catholicism while being incarcerated for a few months during the early war years (for black market activities) with a Polish Catholic priest. This knowledge was to be crucial in enabling him to pass as a Christian.

Perhaps because of their religious agnosticism, Michael and Shlomo were not fatalistic about God's role in helping them survive the war. Michael says that "not for a moment did I think about religion while I was in the camps." Shlomo remarks, "I did not depend on some supreme being to save me. I was banking on myself, on acting properly at the right time, taking the chances, and having a little luck."

During their youth both brothers also participated in Zionist youth groups, Michael in the left-wing Ha-Shomer ha-Tsa'ir and Shlomo in the right-wing Betar.[16] Shlomo observes, "I was more interested in Zionism [than Judaism], and I was an active member of Betar, which leaned to the right of the Zionist movement. In 1936 I trained in a camp run by the Irgun Tseva'i Le'ummi [an underground Jewish military organization] and had intentions to go to Palestine to fight the British for an independent Jewish state. But

LIVERPOOL JOHN MOORES UNIVERSITY
LEARNING SERVICES

these plans did not materialize because of the war." However, the training he received with the Irgun helped prepare him for his later wartime experience with the Polish Partisans.

Memories of Poland retain their quality as emotional reminders for both Michael and Shlomo, although the brothers differ considerably in how they remember the country of their birth. Shlomo has nothing positive to say about his former country. "I remember when we rode our bicycles out into the countryside, the Polish kids would run up to us to 'smell the Jews,' as they said, and to throw rocks at us. . . . I have no desire to ever go back to visit Poland. I dislike the Poles. It's unfortunate that I think that way, but I have to be truthful. In Poland at that time there were many Nazi sympathizers. I am convinced that without the Polish people's cooperation, Germany could not have accomplished what it did. Because even if Jews hid out someplace, the Poles helped the Germans find them." This attitude stems in part from the fact that Shlomo's subsequent survival outside of the camps exposed him even more than Michael to the actions of anti-Semitic Poles. As Sophie Caplan observes, it was (and is) easier for some Polish Jews to accept the fact that "the German Nazis were their absolute enemies and that only evil could be expected from them. The Poles, on the other hand, were their neighbors, their classmates, people with whom they worked and interacted in their daily life, and who now, they felt, betrayed them."[17]

In contrast to Shlomo, Michael retains many fond memories of his family life and youth in Krosno. He especially remembers the Shabbes meals, the Pesach seders, and the Hanukkah gelt he received on each of the eight nights. He recalls with great pleasure playing soccer, ice-skating, skiing cross-country, and swimming in the river that flowed through the town. Michael still remembers the summer vacation he spent with his mother at a Szczawnica resort in the Pieniny Mountains when he was just six years old, the six weeks of summer camp he enjoyed in the majestic Tatra Mountains in the Zakopane region, and a time he spent at the Dunajec River when he was a young member of Ha-Shomer ha-Tsa'ir. He recalls how he was proud of the paramilitary training he received from a Polish Army officer in school and how much he enjoyed the occasional sharpshooting with live ammunition. He also "can picture in my mind the parades we had on Polish national holidays and the military-style march I participated in on Independence Day, how proud I was when the the Polish officer who was leading us gave the command to 'present arms,' and how I executed this command with a rifle of pre–World War I vintage that was nearly as long as my entire body."

Michael even comes to the defense of some Poles. As he says, "It doesn't sit well with me when I hear remarks by other Jews who speak ill of *all* Poles — that 'the Poles were worse than the Germans.' These remarks slander the many righteous and compassionate Poles who tried to help the Jews." But Michael does express considerable resentment toward the Polish-Ukrainian population.

> The Ukrainians are an entirely different story. During World War II they committed many atrocities and were instrumental in rounding up both Jewish and non-Jewish Poles for forced labor and deportations to death camps. Although the Ukrainians were Polish citizens, there was a lot of tension between them and the rest of the population. They considered themselves an independent nationality and were unhappy about being divided between Poland and the Soviet Union. During the war they aligned themselves with Germany under the false belief that if Germany defeated Poland and the Soviet Union, they would be able to acquire an independent state.

THE BEGINNING OF THE WAR

Barney Glaser and Anselm Strauss define a "status passage" as a "movement into a different part of a social structure." They note that such passages may be either "desirable" or "undesirable," for they often entail "a loss or gain of privilege, influence, or power."[18] The Nazi invasion and military defeat of Poland in September 1939 initiated the major epiphany that propelled Polish Jews through an undesirable status passage that would forever change their lives, if they lived at all.

Michael recalls one event that preceded the moment of this status passage. Joshua, his older brother, had completed a term in the Polish military service in the latter part of 1938. As Germany threatened to invade Poland in the summer of 1939, Joshua was recalled to active duty during a massive mobilization of the Polish armed forces. Michael remembers the day, in August 1939, "when I went with my father and Joshua to our rabbi, who gave Joshua a blessing before he was mobilized and recalled to his unit."

However, the moment of Michael's passage into another life came at 5:00 A.M. on September 1, when he was awakened by heavy explosions:

> The military airfield on the outskirts of Krosno was bombed by the German Air Force without any warning. Our planes were destroyed on the ground before they were able to take off. Hours later the Polish radio announced that we had been attacked and that German troops had crossed the Polish border. All males eighteen years and older were ordered to get ready to defend the country. However, the Polish officials miscalculated their defense plans, for our military was no match for the Germans. Our equipment was of World War I vintage. As brave as our men were, the Polish military could not hold the modern German tanks. Our air force was destroyed in the first hours of the war, and within a week the Polish Army began retreating from the western front.

At the same time the Soviet Union, which had signed a nonaggression pact with Germany on August 23, invaded Poland from the east on September 17. Thus, the Polish Army was caught between two foreign military forces. But as Michael recalls:

> At home we were still unaware of these events. A few days after the war had begun, Polish radio ordered all remaining military-age males to follow the retreating Polish Army to the east. Shlomo and I, along with a group of our friends, packed a few pieces of clothing and started a long march on foot to eastern Poland. We walked for five days covering over two hundred kilometers. Several times we were bombarded by the Germans in airplanes. They seemed to make a sport out of it. Flying low, undaunted by any resistance, they shot at us with machine guns, completely disregarding the fact that we were actually civilians. On the fifth day of our journey, while we were traveling off of the main highway, we saw tanks bypassing us. We met up with some Polish soldiers who were roaming the countryside without leadership. They informed us that the enemy had advanced ahead of us and that the war was lost. Thus, there was no longer any reason for us to continue. We entered a small farm, where we bought some food and spent the night sleeping in the barn.

The following morning we started our walk back home. There were thousands of people going in all directions, some going east, some going west. Everybody wanted to be reunited with their families. The Germans had granted the Ukrainians police powers in the towns, and we heard stories about atrocities that civilian Ukrainians were committing against Poles, especially against Jews. It appeared that they felt that they had been liberated by the Germans. They began looting and killing, all condoned by the German authorities. Our group decided that it would be safer to act as if we were non-Jewish Poles.

Several times we were stopped by German soldiers. We didn't know what to expect from them, but we had heard that they were harassing Jews and even killing them right on the spot. They questioned us as to who we were and where we were going. Very few Poles spoke German, but Shlomo knew a little, so we elected him to be our spokesman. He spoke in broken German and explained that we had been separated from our families and were returning home. He told them that we were German nationals who had been living in Poland for generations and that we had escaped from the Polish authorities when they wanted to draft us into the Polish Army to fight Germany. They believed our story and let us go.

One time when we were stopped by some German soldiers, we were searched. I had a metal cigarette case in the inside pocket of my coat. The soldier who searched me thought I was armed and immediately pointed a gun at my head and told me to take it out. This was the first time something like this had ever happened to me. I took the cigarette case out and handed it to him. He kept it.

When we reached the town of Sanok, which was about forty kilometers east of Krosno, we entered a school building to stay the night. A curfew order had been issued, and civilians seen out after dark were to be shot. In late evening we were visited by a German MP [military policeman]. He questioned us, in German, as to who we were. Shlomo appeared to convince the officer of our story. He acted friendly toward us and promised to return in the morning by 7:00 A.M. and provide us with transportation back home. We did not trust him, however, and we left the school building by 6:00 A.M. and started on foot back home.

When we arrived in Krosno, we felt great excitement about being reunited with our family. We hadn't slept in a bed for over two weeks, and it felt great to be home! Unfortunately, this was only a temporary reprieve. Our condition soon changed from bad to worse. Following the German combat troops, the Gestapo came into our town and established a command office less than a block from our home. Every day they issued different orders for the civilian population. It was evident that they were going to be especially hard on Jewish people.

At the time Germany invaded Poland, it was impossible for anyone to know exactly what the Nazis intended to do to the Jews. Jews had been subjected to discrimination for centuries, and many viewed their experience during the early war years as "a modern variation of older persecutions."[19] As Michael notes, "At this point nobody was aware of what they had in mind for us. After all, who could ever have imagined that they intended to exterminate an entire group of people?" According to some historical accounts, even Hitler may not have envisioned the "final solution" of extermination at that time, and the decision to exterminate *all* Jews did not emerge until the latter half of 1941.[20]

By mid-September Poland had been effectively divided between Germany and the Soviet Union, and a border had been established on the San River, about forty kilometers east of Krosno. By the end of the month the Gestapo had begun encouraging Jews to move to the Soviet side. At that time emigration, not extermination, was the predominant Nazi strategy of removing Jews from Germany and its occupied territories. Because transportation was not provided and means of survival were unsure, the Berger family decided that it would be too difficult for the parents to leave. As Michael recounts:

> We faced a dilemma. All signs indicated that it would be better to live under the Soviets than under the Germans. We discussed the situation with our parents and decided it was impossible for our parents to leave home without any transportation. So at the urging of our parents, Shlomo and I decided to go. We hoped that the Germans would not harm any of the older people or small children who were left behind. How wrong we were. My oldest brother, Moishe, chose not to leave home and remained with our parents and our sister Bertha, her husband, Rafael Jakubowicz, and their two daughters, Sonia (age eleven) and Mania (age seven). There was a tearful parting, and we hoped that we would be reunited soon. At this point we did not know what had happened to our brother Joshua, whether he was alive, a war prisoner, or dead at the front. This caused my parents much grief, and they kept praying that he would return safe.

Shlomo and I joined with a few other boys and started on our way by foot to Soviet-occupied Poland. We crossed the River San and spent a few days in a small border village. Then we took a train further east to Sambor, a medium-sized city in eastern Poland. My first impressions of the Soviet occupation were fairly favorable. I did not detect any anti-Semitism among the soldiers, and I felt that if we had to be occupied by a foreign army, I much preferred the Soviets over the Germans. There was no forced labor and no shootings of innocent civilians. But while we were happy to have left the German side, my brother and I felt sad that we had become refugees. We felt like orphans, and we missed our parents, our home, and everything that goes with it.

We slept in a vacated schoolhouse for a few nights but were quickly running low on money and food. Fortunately, I met a Jewish girl who was about a year younger than me who took us to her home to meet her parents. Her family befriended us and invited us to stay with them. They owned a small grocery store and had no problem supplying themselves with food. Thus, we had enough to eat and a place to sleep for awhile.

We began looking around for ways to make money. We knew how to speak a little Ukrainian and were thus able to communicate reasonably well with the Soviet soldiers. There was a shortage of goods in the stores, and a black market was flourishing. Everyone was buying and selling to the Soviet soldiers, who were sending everything they could get a hold of in Poland back to the Soviet Union. We soon realized that the Soviet standard of living lagged behind that of prewar Poland. It was very disheartening to me, for I had believed that people were better off in a socialist country. But while the soldiers had plenty of money and were eager to spend it, there were few commodities available in the Soviet Union to buy. So the Soviet soldiers bought most anything on the black market, from dry goods to jewelry. I remember being amused by the wives of Soviet officers, who had never seen nightgowns before. They wore these nightgowns outside in public, thinking they were wearing fancy evening dresses.

We soon discovered that whatever we were able to buy on the black market, we were able to sell at a profit to the Soviet soldiers. The soldiers were especially crazy about watches. I bought some watches on the black market that were not even working properly and sold them out in the street. I remember one time an officer approached me and asked me how much I wanted for a watch. I quoted him a price; I don't remember exactly how much. He wanted to know if it worked. I shook

it up a little, got it to run, and put it to his ear. He gave me the money
and hurried off thinking he had gotten a bargain.

In addition to their black market activities, Shlomo was able to
supplement their income by working as a tailor. They were doing
reasonably well when, as Michael recalls,

we learned that you could purchase a lot of goods in Lvov, a larger city
nearby, and we began making trips there by train. In Lvov I would
watch for lines of people. Wherever there was a line, I would get in it,
not even knowing what they were selling. One time I stood in line all
night, and when they opened the store in the morning, I found out
they were selling material for suits and other clothing. I bought three
and one-half yards of nice wool cloth, enough to make a man's suit. It
cost me about 70 złotys, and I sold it back in Sambor for 190.

One day as Shlomo and I were boarding the train to Lvov, we heard
our names called. We turned around and saw our missing brother,
Joshua, still in Polish military uniform. He had been taken prisoner by
the Soviet Army and was being marched east toward Soviet Russia. He
had managed to escape and had taken a train going west — hence our
surprise meeting. We were all overwhelmed with happiness and
wished we could let our parents know that Joshua was alive and well.
But there was no way to communicate with them, for there was no
mail going between the Soviet and German sides.

On another day two friends and I returned to Lvov because we had
heard that the Russian authorities were registering Poles to work in the
coal mines in Soviet Russia. We stood outside all night in the cold to
wait for the registration office to open. In the morning a Russian military officer who was Jewish spoke to us in Yiddish. He accepted my
two friends but wouldn't take me. My friends were over six feet tall and
looked like men, but I was too short [five feet, four inches]. The Russian told me that I wasn't strong enough and discouraged me from registering. He made fun of me, telling me I "wouldn't last a week," and
told me to go home.

On returning to Sambor, Michael developed a bad cold, flu, and
heavy cough. Shlomo and Joshua decided that he needed the care of
their mother and the comforts of home, and they did not want the
responsibility of looking after a sick sibling. But it had become more
difficult to cross the border between the German and Soviet sides

because tensions between Germany and the Soviet Union were already heightening. According to Michael:

> We heard that there were Poles who, for a fee, would smuggle Jews across the River San from one side of the border to the other. My brothers hired a Pole who agreed to escort me and another boy from our town, who still had a sister living in Krosno. On New Year's Eve, when we figured that the soldiers on both sides of the border would be partying, we crossed the frozen river into German-occupied Poland. The smuggler took us to a house where we spent the night. The next morning, after we ate, we left without the smuggler and hitched a ride on a truck the remaining forty kilometers to Krosno.

Michael remembers this as a fatal mistake, a case where a decision to act, to exercise agency, did not have its intended results. "My parents were elated to see me, but it soon became obvious to me that it had been a mistake to return. The atmosphere was much more repressive than when I had left. There were Gestapo on every corner, and Jews had been ordered to wear armbands marked with the star of David."

Three to four weeks later Shlomo and Joshua returned with plans of bringing the whole family back to the Russian side. "We were finally reunited with our family. Our parents thought it was a miracle that Joshua had survived combat and that we had met him under such circumstances. We planned to wait until the weather was warmer and then arrange for smugglers to take the whole family to the Soviet side, even if it meant abandoning everything, our home and personal possessions. This we were never able to do. The borders were being guarded more closely, and it became impossible for us to cross back to the Soviet side."

The Berger family (1921) prior to Michael's birth. *Above, left to right,* Bertha, Rosa (mother), Shlomo; *below, left to right,* Joshua, Moishe, Jacob (father), Rose.

The four Berger brothers: Michael, Shlomo, Moishe, Joshua.

Michael as a youth.

The Krosno Gideon Sports Club: Joshua (far left), Michael (to right of Joshua), Shlomo (second to right, front standing).

The Berger family tailor shop: Joshua (front left), Michael (next to Joshua), Shlomo (back left), and employees.

Nieces Sonia and Mania.

Shlomo and Mania.

Joshua in Polish Army uniform.

CHAPTER 3

Living Under German Occupation in a Small Town

In the early part of 1940 the Nazis intensified their anti-Jewish campaign in Krosno, although their systematic program of extermination could still not have been imagined by its potential victims. In fact, the inconsistency of the Nazis' treatment of Jews made realistic appraisal of the situation difficult. According to Michael:

The iron hand of the Gestapo tightened with every coming day. There was always a new danger, and we never knew what was waiting for us the next hour. At one time everything could be going smoothly, without incident. We were even able to go to synagogue or have prayer meetings. But the next minute there would be a raid, and people would be grabbed by the Gestapo and disappear. This inconsistency prevented us from running, hiding, or fighting back and gave us hope that our plight was only temporary. I believe the Germans did this on purpose to confuse and delude us.

I remember occasions when we even socialized with a German police officer. At the time there were Jewish refugees from Łódź who had been resettled to Krosno.[1] Most of them lived in the synagogue, but some managed to get rooms with other families. There was one family that consisted of a father, mother, and two beautiful daughters. A German officer liked these girls and protected them. We used to go to their home and have parties when this German officer, who allowed us to have a good time, was present. We would sing, tell jokes and stories, and read books together. There was also another very pretty girl from Łódź who had a number of German admirers. She spent many nights in the homes of German officers, who lavished her with gifts, even though it was a capital offense for Jews and Germans to have sexual relations with each other. Yet the Germans disobeyed their own laws. It always amazed me how they could be fond of some of our Jewish girls and yet want to abuse or kill the rest of us.

ESCALATING REPRESSION

The Gestapo established a local Jewish Council through which it issued orders to the Jewish population and a Jewish police force to implement these orders. In this way the Jews' relationship with their oppressors was mediated by other Jews. Even though the Berger family did not attempt to flee or go into hiding, it did resist Nazi edicts whenever it could. One of the first instances of resistance involved an order for Jews to deliver all pieces of jewelry, gold, and silver to the German authorities. As Michael recounts:

Any Jew found disobeying these orders faced immediate execution by shooting. I remember that my mother owned a large silver candelabra that had taken her many years of saving to buy. It had been every married Jewish woman's ambition to own such a candelabra with which to light candles on the Shabbes and on holidays. My mother just couldn't turn it over to the Germans, so she gave it to a Polish girlfriend. At that time she assumed that the girlfriend would only have to temporarily keep it for us. This was our first act of defiance living under the German occupation.

A week later the Gestapo demanded all articles made of copper, which the Germans recycled and used for war materials. All we had was a coffeemaker [bean grinder], which we delivered. Next they demanded all furs, including fur collars that we had to rip off from our overcoats. These items were sent to Germany to be used by German military personnel and civilians. The following day you could see Jewish people wearing their coats without collars. Many of us sewed old blankets into our coats to keep us warm. My mother gave her coat to a girlfriend.

I remember one time after a deadline for delivering fur materials had passed, we realized that we had not turned over a sheep vest that we owned. We decided to burn it in our old wood-burning oven. It was a winter night, and outside you could smell the burning vest. The Gestapo headquarters was less than a block away, and we were extremely anxious and tense that night, fearing that if we were discovered, this little act of defiance could have cost us our lives.

Daily orders were also given to the Jewish Council to deliver a certain amount of Jews for forced labor. Every morning the able-bodied men and women in Krosno were marched out under armed guard to work. We shoveled snow from the highways, cleaned the city streets, worked at the airfield, and loaded and unloaded coal in the train depot. We labored for ten to twelve hours a day. Some Jews who possessed special skills — like electricians, automobile repairmen, carpenters, tailors, and shoemakers — were treated a little better since all German personnel required their services, often for their own personal benefit. Because our family owned a tailor shop and many Germans, including Gestapo officers, enjoyed our free services, for awhile we did not have it as bad as some other Jewish families.

Although Berger family members were able to exchange their tailoring resources with the Gestapo to achieve some temporary amelioration of the family's condition (and, as we shall see, were aided by persons who had connections with the authorities), they resisted the temptation to seek favors by cooperating with the Nazis themselves. As Michael explains:

I was very resentful of the Jews who cooperated with the Nazis. There were a few boys I had grown up with who joined the Jewish police and helped the Gestapo round up Jews for forced labor. I would never have joined them! At one time Shlomo was thinking of becoming a policeman. Our entire family opposed this, and we told him that he would be an outcast if he did. He listened to us and did not join. Of course, at that time it was not clear what kind of "dirty work" one would be asked to do for the Gestapo. I suppose you can't blame some Jews for hoping that they could minimize the hardship for themselves and their families if they helped the Nazis. But this type of cooperation went against my grain, and I would never have participated in it. I was more defiant. I knew that becoming a policeman could force you to become a collaborator, even if unwillingly. There was one boy in Krosno, the son of a Jewish baker, who became a policeman. He was forced to put his own father on a truck for deportation.

The armband order that had been issued was designed to prevent Jews from mingling with or hiding among the non-Jewish population. Noncompliance was punishable by death. However, my friends and I often disregarded this order, removed our armbands, and rode our bicycles or even took a train to nearby towns to visit relatives or make some transactions in the black market. In spite of our defiant attitude, we always feared being recognized by Poles, many of whom reported Jews to the Gestapo. They did this for money, rewards, or plain anti-Semitism. The Germans in their cunning way were successful at dividing the population. The propaganda newspapers were convincing the Poles that they had lost their country because of an international Jewish conspiracy and that the Jews were the cause of the war. In their ignorance many Poles believed the propaganda, only later to discover that after there were no more Jews to deport, the Germans intensified their repression of Poles by conducting house and street raids and deporting them to Germany for forced labor.

One time a friend and I rode our bikes about fifteen kilometers to the nearby town of Rymanów to buy pepper on the black market. We arranged a purchase of two fifty-pound sacks at a tavern owned by my mother's uncle. As we were getting ready to leave the next day, a Polish-Ukrainian police officer appeared. Someone must have reported us to him, for when he started to question us, it was obvious that he knew what we were up to. This officer, however, had a reputation for taking bribes. He threatened to arrest us, but when my uncle offered him a beer and then some money, he left us alone. We loaded the sacks of pepper on our bikes and rode back to Krosno. Luckily no one spotted us. When we returned to Krosno, we sold the pepper to another black marketer for a profit.

Like Michael, Shlomo recalls experiences dealing in the black market. One incident in November 1940, though dangerous, taught him valuable cultural knowledge that later helped him survive passing as a Catholic Pole:

I went to the city of Tarnów to buy American dollars from a dollar dealer. There on the street I met a friend whom I knew from an Irgun training camp. He asked me what I was doing in Tarnów, and I told him I was buying dollars. He asked when I was leaving to go home and said he would like to see me off at the railway station. I told him that I was going back on the afternoon train. When I arrived at the station, he was there to greet me. After we said good-bye to each other, he left, and a plainclothes Gestapo officer walked over and arrested me. I suspected that this so-called friend was an informer and that he had pointed me out to the Gestapo, for there was no other reason for them to stop me.

I was searched for American dollars, but I had been careful not to carry any with me. The dealer had sent his twelve-year-old daughter with me, and she was carrying the money. When the Gestapo arrested me, they also arrested her. But the Gestapo officials wanted to keep the money, and I later found out that they let her go so there wouldn't be any record of her arrest. I was interrogated by two Gestapo men and beaten for over two hours, but I denied any involvement with foreign currencies. They said, "That is enough for today. We'll start again tomorrow," and they left me lying on the floor, black and blue all over.

I was in a second-story room with an iron-barred window that had a circle in the middle that was facing the street. I was very skinny and tried to put my head through it. I took off my coat — it was winter — and squeezed through the hole in the center. I let myself down on the gutter to the street and ran, not knowing where. I saw a girl on the street wearing a Jewish armband. I approached her and asked her to take me to her house. She did, and I hid out in her family's house for a couple of weeks. I wore women's clothes and even a wig — the women were wearing wigs at that time — just in case. I also sent word to my parents to let them know where I was.

Shlomo's mother was able to arrange for his release by passing a bribe through someone she knew who had connections with the Gestapo. He was able to return home to Krosno. However, according to Shlomo:

A few weeks later a Gestapo official named Becker, who had a reputation as a murderer, came to our house. He knew us personally, for the Gestapo headquarters was just around the corner from our home and we used to make clothes for them. Becker said to me, "Well, Shlomo, get your clothes." He took me over to the headquarters, and the Gestapo commandant said, "That's him? What did you do that they arrested you and you escaped?" I replied, "I don't know. I was just stopped without any reason. And I was beaten up and just couldn't take it. When I got a chance, I escaped." He said, "Well, you won't do it again." Apparently he didn't know what I had been arrested for, but he had an order to rearrest me. He was very polite, but he went ahead and put handcuffs on me, put me in a car, and drove me to the nearby town of Jasło, where I was imprisoned in a jail without a hearing.

As it turned out, this was a fortuitous experience, for Shlomo was placed in a cell with about a dozen Polish political prisoners, including a Roman Catholic priest who conducted religious services three times a day. Thus, a mishap turned into a resource as Shlomo had the opportunity to learn about religious rituals and customs that later enabled him to pass as a Christian Pole.

In the spring of 1941 Shlomo was called into the office at the jail. As he recalls:

> There was a German officer, not a Gestapo man, who said he was in charge of foreign currencies. He read me a document that said I had been dealing in American dollars, that I had been arrested by the Gestapo in Tarnów, and that I had escaped and been rearrested. He wanted me to sign a confession. I told him that the charges were not true. He replied that for every lie I would tell him, I would receive twenty-five lashes over my back with a rubber stick. I still refused, so he told me to lie down, and he counted out twenty-five. I admitted that I had been arrested and escaped but insisted that I hadn't been dealing in dollars. He gave me another twenty-five lashes. I remember him counting to twenty-five four times, and I still would not sign. Finally he said if I wouldn't sign the confession, he was going to put me back into the cell. I asked him what would happen to me if I signed. He said he would release me and told me my mother was waiting outside. Apparently she had again arranged to pay off the Gestapo in exchange for my release if I signed a confession. Finally I agreed to sign the confession. I was put back in the cell but was released the next day. After that I returned home and worked daily, without pay, in different assigned places — shoveling snow and carrying bricks to the airport and railway.

THE FINAL DAYS

Michael and Shlomo concluded their narrative account of this phase of their experience by reconstructing the events that culminated in the liquidation of the Jewish community in Krosno,[2] the death of their parents, and Michael's deportation to an SS military camp at Moderówka. According to Michael:

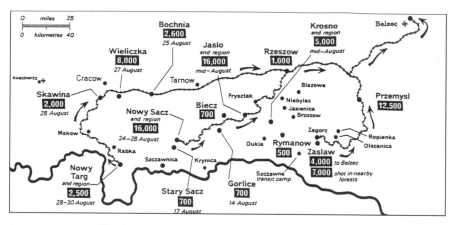

Deportations to Bełżec from western Galacia region of Poland, August 1942. Copyright ©
Martin Gilbert, *Atlas of the Holocaust* (2nd ed.), William Morrow, New York, New York, 1993.

The Gestapo, with the help of their Ukrainian allies, began conducting
random raids and deportations of both Jews and Poles to concentration
camps. The first people who were the main victims of these policies
were the intelligentsia, including Jews and non-Jews, for the Germans
desired to maintain a noneducated Polish population. All this was done
under the guise of "resettlement." People deported to concentration
camps and later to gas chambers were led to believe that they were
being resettled in different areas where housing and work would be
provided. This helps explain the lack of resistance. By the time these
unfortunate people realized their fate, it was too late to resist or escape.
People simply disappeared without a trace.

On June 22, 1941, Germany suddenly broke their nonaggression
pact with the Soviet Union and invaded Soviet Russia. They quickly
pushed the Soviets out of Polish territories and advanced into the Soviet
Union to within forty kilometers of Moscow. Now all Jews from eastern Poland as well as western Poland found themselves under German
domination. In December of 1941 the tide turned on the Russian
front. The Soviet Army stiffened their resistance and stopped the German advance. This made the Germans furious, bolder, and meaner.
They began executing people in open daylight on city streets. No German official needed any justification for killing non-German civilians.
Each dispensed justice according to his own mood or whim.

The first major liquidation of Krosno Jews occurred on August 10, 1942. Both brothers remember this Holocaust epiphany as the most traumatic day of their entire ordeal. As Shlomo recalls:

All Jews regardless of age had to report at the marketplace near the railroad station for a "registration." Each Jew was told they could bring up to twenty-five pounds of personal possessions. We were to leave our homes and apartments unlocked and available for police inspection. Anyone found in their homes after 9:00 A.M. would be shot on sight. Panic erupted! Some people tried to escape, but most of those who did were caught and shot. The Ukrainian troops did most of the killing for the Germans.

As the people were assembled in the marketplace, numerous trucks with SS and Gestapo, German civilian police, and Polish and Ukrainian officers arrived and encircled the area so that no one could escape. We were ordered by the Gestapo to line up and get ready for "registration." Next Gestapo officers began segregating the assembled people into different groups. Older people, men and women, were moved to one side and forced into several large army trucks. They were brutally beaten, and those who were not able to climb on the truck under their own power were simply picked up and thrown on top. One young pretty girl stepped out of line to plead with a Gestapo officer to release her elderly mother. He ordered the girl to get into the truck with her mother. She pleaded with him, but he would not let her remain with the group that was still standing. After several trucks filled with the older people were loaded, they departed under heavy guard with machine guns mounted on accompanying vehicles. My father was among them! At the time we had no idea where they were taken. Later we learned that they were all delivered to a forest outside the village of Barwinek and shot in front of previously prepared mass graves. Nobody came back alive.

To this account Michael adds his vivid recollection of his father's last words as he was put on to the truck that would take him to his death: "Children, save yourselves!" Gallant and Cross note that a "challenged identity" that gave Jews the will to go on in spite of their suffering derived in part from others' response to their common ordeal.[3] Perhaps in his moment of death, Jacob Berger helped his sons maintain their will to live.

LIVERPOOL
JOHN MOORES UNIVERSITY
TRUEMAN STREET LIBRARY
TEL. 051 231 4022/4023

After their father was taken away, the brothers tried in vain to protect their mother, sister, and niece from experiencing a similar fate. As Michael recounts:

> Within hours the trucks, now empty, returned to Krosno. Representatives of various German military services arrived and selected a group of young people whom they needed for forced labor and skilled work, mostly in the military airfield. These people were loaded into trucks and driven to previously prepared barracks. An official of Organisation Todt [a German military construction agency][4] who was in charge of military supplies [not weaponry] asked and received permission from the Gestapo to release into his custody the four Berger brothers, our brother-in-law Rafael, and our niece Sonia [who looked older than her age] to work under his supervision. We pleaded with him to allow our mother, sister Bertha, and young niece Mania to come with us. But he refused. They were left behind as we were taken to work in a Todt supply warehouse.
>
> That night we did not return to our home but were led to a ghetto that had been created in a one-block area of the town that had been known as the "egg place." The ghetto consisted of four houses and two three-story and one single-story apartments which housed about eight hundred people, with fifteen to twenty people per room. People slept three high on boxes and boards and on the floor. It was incredibly bad. Guards were posted outside the ghetto, and nobody was allowed to leave without special permission.

Shlomo recalls being assigned to a room in the ghetto with about ten other young people, but Michael recollects merely finding a place to sleep. In either case the next morning they were led under armed guard to work in the family's tailor shop, which had been taken over by a Pole, to make uniforms for Todt and civilian clothes for the personal use of the chief Todt official and his wife. That morning they also learned what had happened to the Jews who had still been in the marketplace after the six family members had been removed, including their immediate family, numerous relatives, and close friends. According to Shlomo:

> They were standing all day, dehydrated from the heat, without even a drop of water to drink, and they were severely beaten by the Gestapo. At the end of the day they were led to the railroad station and loaded

into closed freight cars with about sixty people per car. The train left eastward the next morning. While we do not know for sure, we suspect that they were taken to Be*l*żec to be gassed. We do know from a Polish person who was paid by the surviving Jews to follow the train that the train had been standing locked all day at the nearby Iwonicz railway station. People were crying for water and nobody responded. Dr. Baumring, a prominent local Jewish physician, called out from the train to the German guards, "You are barbarians!" The guards dragged him from the car and shot him.

At the time Michael felt that "although we were working in our old tailor shop, everything had been taken away from us. All that remained of our family were the four brothers, Rafael, and Sonia. We were overwhelmed with grief! I could not sleep. My heart ached! I could not believe that this could happen in the twentieth century. All that we had left was a temporary reprieve for ourselves and the hope that we might survive."

In the early part of September the Gestapo ordered the Krosno Jewish Council to deliver all the remaining Jewish tailors for transportation to an SS military camp to make uniforms for the Ukrainian troops. The camp was located about fifteen kilometers from Krosno in Moderówka. Michael remembers trying to convince the Jewish Council to allow the four Berger brothers to remain in Krosno:

We tried to tell them that we still had work to complete for different German officials, but they said that they had to deliver at least thirty tailors to the Germans. They eventually compromised and agreed to allow two of us to stay to finish the work if two would go to the camp. We had a family meeting to decide who would go and who would stay. Shlomo and Joshua were the most experienced tailors among us. We also felt that Shlomo was the most aggressive and the one who would best be able to act in ways that would maximize his chances of survival outside of the camps. He knew a boy our age named Nagel who worked in the German store in the Gestapo building. Nagel had connections with a Jewish printer who did the printing and made official seals for the Gestapo. This printer had made an extra seal that he used to stamp forged documents, which he made available to Jews for a price. Thus, we decided that Moishe and I would go to the Moderówka camp and that Shlomo and Joshua would try to get all of us false identity papers with Polish surnames and the printer's stamp. Then we would all try to escape into non-Jewish cities to survive the war by any means we could. Unfortunately, we were never able to carry out these plans.

After Michael and Moishe were sent to the Moderówka camp, Shlomo recalls that another "registration" was announced through the Jewish Council, with a promise by the Gestapo that all Jews who had hidden and not appeared for the August 10 registration would be issued legalization papers and permitted to stay in the ghetto. "About two hundred people showed up at the specified time. At first the Gestapo officers behaved very humanely. But as soon as they were convinced that no one else would come, they began beating people with rifles and clubs and forcing them on to trucks. They were driven away to an unknown place, where they were undoubtedly killed."

CHAPTER 4

Surviving Outside the Camps

Shlomo and Joshua remained in Krosno until the final liquidation of the Krosno ghetto, which occurred on December 2, 1942. On that day the remaining Jews were loaded into trucks and transported to a larger ghetto in Rzeszów, about fifty kilometers away. In the process many were beaten and shot, among them the town rabbi. This day marked the end of the Jewish community that had lived in Krosno for many generations.

Before the liquidation Shlomo had been able to get the false identity papers through Nagel, but he was unable to help Michael and Moishe. With the identity papers in hand, Shlomo, Joshua, Rafael, and Sonia decided it would be best to separate and attempt to flee in order to avoid being shot or deported to a concentration camp. According to Shlomo:

> The day before the liquidation we noticed several Gestapo men arriving from a neighboring town. We suspected that something ominous was about to happen. When Nagel came into the tailor shop saying that he had heard this, too, we decided not to go back that night to sleep in the ghetto. Each of us decided to hide out for the night wherever we could. We planned that if on the next day the Gestapo seemed to be preparing to round up Jews, we would leave by train eastward and try to survive as Poles with our false identification papers.
>
> I don't know where the others went that night. After dark I slipped out of the ghetto and went to the home of the Pole who had taken over our tailor shop. I told him I intended to sleep there that night, whether

he liked it or not. He reluctantly let me in, and I slept in the attic. Perhaps he took sympathy on me, for it was winter and very cold. The next morning the Pole went out to see what was happening in the ghetto. He came back and reported that "the ghetto is surrounded. Trucks are pulling up. They are beating and shooting Jews. They're going to liquidate the ghetto!" He told me that I had to leave. I said that I wasn't leaving until nightfall. He replied, "What do you mean? I'm going to throw you out. I'm not going to take a chance with my life." I said, "You just try to put me out now, and I'm going to tell the Gestapo that you hid me overnight. And then we'll both be in trouble. But I promise you that the minute it gets dark, I will leave." Thus, he had no choice, and I hid in the attic the rest of the day.

Previously Shlomo had been given an address by one of his father's former Polish customers, Mrs. Tadeusz Duchowski. Her husband was now working as a supervisor with a construction crew that was on location rebuilding bridges in Czortków and Niźniów, two towns that were about ninety kilometers east of the city of Stanisławów. Shlomo recalls, "Mrs. Duchowski came into the tailor shop. I didn't know her very well, but we started a conversation. I don't remember if I asked her for help or if she offered on her own.[1] But she told me that 'if something goes wrong, go and see my husband.' She gave me the address where I could find him and asked me to memorize it so there would be nothing written down. I had never heard of Czortków or Niźniów, which were about seven to eight hours by train from Krosno, but going there seemed the best chance that I had."

Earlier I indicated that research on Christians who helped Jews during the Holocaust has found that these Christians were more likely than those who did not help to have had prior relationships with Jews.[2] Researchers have also described helpers in terms of possessing personal attributes such as empathy and individuality and as having a prior commitment to helping the needy. Certainly anti-Nazi sentiments were a factor for many who gave aid. However, Shlomo remains uncertain as to why the Duchowskis were willing to help him. "I don't really know why they helped. Mrs. Duchowski was a very nice person, and perhaps she just liked me or felt sorry for me. I knew nothing about Mr. Duchowski, except that before the war he had been a football [soccer] player and a member of an anti-Semitic political party [Endek]."

With the forged documents that he had obtained through Nagel from the local printer, Shlomo walked about eight kilometers, accompanied by Mrs. Duchowski, through snow-covered fields to a dimly lit and unguarded train station at Iwonicz. As Shlomo describes the experience:

> I didn't dare to go to the Krosno station. But there were no Gestapo or other police at the Iwonicz station. I bought a ticket and boarded a train heading east. Joshua and I had planned to meet each other later. But this never happened. After the war I was told by other survivors who knew him that he had been rounded up in a street raid in Lvov with other non-Jewish Poles who were going to be deported to Germany for slave labor. He, however, knew that during a physical examination it would be discovered that he was a Jew and that he would be shot. In those days in Europe only Jewish males were circumcised. Apparently Joshua managed to escape and ended up in a ghetto in the eastern Polish town of Kołomyja. This ghetto was eventually liquidated and no one survived. Later I was also told that Rafael and Sonia were taken to a ghetto in Rzeszów and later to Bełżec where they were killed.

PASSING AS A POLE

Shlomo's forged documents were, in his words, "rather limited. All I had were two small pieces of paper: one was an identification paper with a false Polish name, Jan Jerzowski, that was certified with a counterfeit Gestapo seal; and the other was a forged Todt work order indicating that I was to report to work near Kiev in the Ukraine. During the time I was traveling on the train, police officers often boarded and asked to look at passengers' documents. Somehow I managed to get through."

Shlomo's escape from Krosno and his new identity were accompanied by a changed "awareness context." Barney Glaser and Anselm Strauss define an "awareness context" as "the total combination of what each interactant knows about the identity of the other and his own identity in the eyes of the other."[3] In Krosno for the most part

Shlomo had acted in an "open" awareness context where the Germans were knowledgeable about his identity. But his new circumstance involved passage into a "closed" awareness context where he concealed his identity from his antagonists. Shlomo's ability to maintain this closed context through a convincing performance as Jan Jerzowski would mark the difference between life and death. However, he could not have done this for very long on his own.

Shlomo rode the train eastward until it stopped at Drohobycz, a town that was midway between Krosno and Lvov. He had to get off the train there and wait about six or seven hours for the next one to depart. As he recalls:

> It was winter and very cold, with lots of snow. I had no luggage or extra clothing with me, just the clothes I was wearing, a pair of boots, and a winter coat. While I was waiting, I started to walk. I didn't know where to go, but I was looking for a place where there were Jews. I noticed a young man about my age wearing a Jewish armband. I asked if he could tell me where the Jewish ghetto was. He said to follow him. There was a ghetto, which, though fenced in, was still easy to get in and out of. Poles were coming in doing business, bringing in food, and buying goods from the Jews. So I followed him into the ghetto. My socks were wet from walking in the snow. I went inside a place, took off my shoes, and dried out my socks. I told this man that I was Jewish and that I wanted to stay there until the next train arrived.

The Jewish stranger accompanied Shlomo back to the train station. His parting words gave Shlomo encouragement: "I just want to tell you that you are going to survive the war. If I didn't recognize you as a Jew, nobody else will either." After this Shlomo boarded the train again and traveled until he approached Stanisławów. He remembers that the train could not continue because the main bridges were out. As he says, "We had to get off and ride horses and buggies across temporary bridges to the other side. Then I boarded another train and traveled to Czortków, where I waited for Mr. Duchowski in front of a small house where he lived."

In most cases Christian aid to Jews during the war had an unplanned beginning.[4] This was certainly true of Tadeusz Duchowski. According to him:

At first I didn't recognize Shlomo because I had dealt mostly with his father. He asked me, "Excuse me, sir. Do you recognize me?" I said, "No, I don't know you. I'm sorry. You do look familiar, but I can't remember where I've seen you." Then Shlomo told me, "You might not remember me, but you do remember my father" and proceeded to explain why he had come to see me and how my wife had said that I might be able to help him.

I took Shlomo to a restaurant and tried to figure out what I could do for him. I told him that there were a lot of unfriendly Ukrainian police in Czortków and that the Gestapo had a training school there for Poles who were of German descent.[5] I explained that Niźniów, which was a smaller town, would be safer. There were a number of Ukrainian police there, but the chances of running into someone who would recognize him would not be as great.

Duchowski, who was a supervisor in his company's office, offered to give Shlomo a cover as a worker but said he couldn't pay Shlomo. Duchowski took Shlomo to the Niźniów police station and helped him register as a company worker and get him a food ration card. Shlomo recalls that

> I worked in the company office and went out on location to the bridge every day. I just tried to look busy, making notes and charts. I had about fifty single-dollar bills that I had saved from my earlier black marketing activities. At that time an American dollar went a long way, and this is how I supported myself. I even did a little tailoring for some of the office employees to make money.
>
> I rented a room in Niźniów with one of the Polish workers. I learned from him that the man who was in charge of the office was the son of a judge who was a Jew who had converted to Catholicism. The son was probably raised as a Christian, but by German criteria he was still Jewish. The people at the office knew who he was, but nobody said anything. One day the two of us were talking. He looked at me suspiciously and started to say, "Are you . . . ?" He didn't even finish his sentence. I said, "Am I what?" He was evasive and I said, "Are you?" We were both uncomfortable, and neither of us admitted what we suspected about each other. But I felt that I knew more about him than he knew about me. Finally he told me, "Let me give you some advice." He said I better correct my pronunciation of certain Polish words because I

wasn't saying them properly. He also told me, "When you drink tea or coffee, don't use cube sugar and don't eat sunflower seeds because these are Jewish customs." Later Mr. Duchowski talked to this man and told him to leave me alone, or his own life would be in danger.

Meanwhile Shlomo lived as a Catholic Pole and concealed his identity from everyone except Duchowski. Shlomo attended church services every day and applied what he had learned about Catholicism while in prison in Jasło. However, as he says, "I never dared to go to confession."

During this time Shlomo also benefited from his friendship with a young Polish woman, Kristina. He convinced her that he was a Polish political refugee and that he needed new documents to survive. According to Shlomo:

> The Gestapo had just issued an order that every Gentile needed a *Kenncarte*, an internal passport issued directly by the Gestapo. However, in order to get a Kenncarte, you had to have a birth certificate. Kristina helped me convince the local priest to issue a birth certificate to me under my assumed name, Jan Jerzowski. On the bottom of the paper he put in tiny letters that the certificate had been issued on the basis of verbal testimony. But I had enough nerve to walk into the Gestapo office with this certificate and ask them to issue me a legitimate internal passport, which they did.

Shlomo recollects that it was about February or March 1943, when the Soviets were starting to advance on the eastern front, that the Polish work crew was relocated somewhere to the west, near Warsaw. He decided not to risk going with the crew but to flee into the forest with other Polish workers from the area who feared being sent to Germany to perform forced slave labor. Shlomo remembers:

> The streets were full of retreating German soldiers, and there was increasing chaos. Mr. Duchowski and I talked about what to do. He told me that he had done all that he could do for me and that it would be too dangerous for me to remain with the company since it was likely that everyone would be searched and personally examined at the new location. I told him that I was grateful to him for helping me and that I could now handle things on my own. I said that I had been thinking of

joining up with the Polish Partisans in the forests, and this is what I now planned to do. He asked me never to reveal that he had helped me. I promised him that I would never put him in jeopardy.

PASSING WITH THE POLISH PARTISANS

Shlomo fled into the forest and joined up with a group of about one hundred anti-Nazi Polish Partisans who hoped to hold out until they could meet up with the advancing Soviet Army. Shlomo recalls:

Most of the Poles in my group came from the region and had parents or relatives in the area. The Polish population supported us with food, but the majority of people in the area were Ukrainians who were pro-German and not friendly to the Partisans. However, we forced them to give us food or simply took it from them if we had to.[6]

Eventually my group grew to about two hundred, but we did not have any experienced officers among us, and we were not very aggressive. The arms we had were mostly from what the Poles had hidden before the war. Occasionally we attacked German military installations or transports, but mostly we were constantly on the run. We thought more of survival than of fighting.

For the most part Shlomo's involvement with the Partisans was, in the context of the war, a desirable status passage. He was still exposed to considerable risk, but he had become part of a collectivity that afforded its members mutual protection against the Germans. However, most Jews who participated in the Partisan movement have reported being attacked or threatened by non-Jewish Partisans.[7] Shlomo was aware of this and thus had to maintain a closed awareness context and conceal his Jewish identity from the other members of his group. According to Shlomo:

The leaders of my group issued me a rifle, which I knew how to use from the time I had trained with the Irgun. However, I never told them I was Jewish because I was fearful of what they would do to me. They often talked about the Jews — that the one good thing that Hitler was doing was killing the Jews. Thus, I always had to remain on guard when I was with them and do things that were against my grain. They drank a lot of homemade vodka that smelled really bad. I didn't like to drink and couldn't hold my liquor. I had to swallow whole glasses of vodka and somehow sneak out to the side and stick my fingers in my mouth and throw it up.

During his time with the Partisans Shlomo remembers a Holocaust epiphany that he experienced as a "crucial moment" in his survival. In the summer of 1943 he was chosen by the leaders of his group to go on a mission to Stanisławów:

I was not privy to the inner circle of my group, but they selected me to get some information about what the Germans were up to. They had learned that a number of SS had recently arrived in Stanisławów, and they wanted to know what this was all about. I think they chose me because I knew a little German. They gave me a counterfeit document on a little piece of paper that said I had been called to the labor department to report. I took a train to Stanisławów, and when we pulled into the station, I noticed that both sides of the railroad tracks were all surrounded with German police. A voice came out through a bullhorn telling everyone to first remain on the train and then to all come out through one of the exits. I figured that this was the end, but I didn't try to hide. I went straight forward and was among the first ones to get out of the train. I walked through the middle of the German police who were standing on both sides of the aisle that had been formed. I came to the front of a door, the exit to the station, where a uniformed Gestapo man and a Ukrainian policeman who spoke Polish were standing. The Gestapo asked me, in German, "Where are you going?" I held out my forged document and the internal passport I had from Niźniów, looked him straight in the eye, and said, in Polish, "I don't understand German." He said again, "What did you come here for?" I repeated, "I don't understand." Then the Ukrainian officer began translating in Polish. I said I had an order from the labor department to appear for registration. The Gestapo took the document and looked it over. He looked at me closely, and I continued to look him straight in the eyes. I died a thousand times at that time. And then he said to me, "Forward." This is one of the experiences that I remember most vividly.

When I was in Stanisławów, I just walked around and observed what was going on. I discovered that the recent influx of SS was due to the increased security that was necessary because of a meeting of high-ranking German officers. Apparently the meeting concerned possible unrest from the Ukrainians. Although the Ukrainians had collaborated with the Germans, they wanted their independence. When they saw that this was not part of the bargain, some began making plans to revolt. I also learned that the officers were preparing the German Army to retreat because of the advances being made by the Soviets.

After this episode Shlomo returned safely to the Partisans and remained with them until meeting up with the Soviet Army toward the end of March 1944. Just before this happened, however, he experienced yet another epiphanic moment, which involved a Hungarian regiment that was fighting alongside the German Army:

The night before the Soviets caught up with us, several of the Partisans, including myself, were caught by the Hungarians. They turned us over to the Germans, who put us in a holding cell that was guarded by a German soldier. They told us that we were going to be executed. This was one of the many times that I thought I had reached the end. But in the middle of the night a group of Hungarian soldiers arrived, killed our guard, and liberated us. Apparently they felt that if the Germans executed us, they would be blamed for it. And the minute the Soviets arrived, the Hungarians threw down their weapons and marched voluntarily into the Soviet prison camp.

PASSING WITH THE SOVIET ARMY

The Holocaust epiphany involving Shlomo's escape from death at the hands of the Hungarian soldiers was an instance of what survivors experienced as the "luck" of survival. Moreover, at this point in his ordeal Shlomo was quite clearly aided by changing external conditions associated with the Soviet war effort that were beyond his sphere of influence. As he recalls:

Soon after we met the Soviet Army, a German counteroffensive forced us to retreat. During this time we were bombed and machine-gunned by diving German planes. I remember lying in a field that was barren from the winter, with my face dug into the ground, and bullets flying all around me. But I wasn't hit. Not even a scratch. These are experiences that stick in your mind. You ask yourself, how did you manage not to get hit by a bomb or bullet or shrapnel?

The German counteroffensive forced us back to Czernowitz in Romania, where we settled for about three months. There we [the Poles] were inducted into the local militia under the command of a Soviet officer. In June when the Soviets began another offensive we were inducted into the Soviet Army.

Although Shlomo continued to benefit from luck, joining the Soviet Army was a desirable status passage that further empowered him. However, his ability to exercise agency to capitalize on this opportunity was a key factor as well. Because of his facility with German and Russian, Shlomo was able to make himself useful to a Soviet officer who was in charge of German prisoners of war. When additional Soviet troops were sent to the front lines, he persuaded the officer to retain him, after offering him a little bribe:

I had a gold watch that I had taken from a German prisoner. When I offered him the watch, he agreed right away, for the Russians were just crazy about watches. But in order to keep me, he had to give me a rank, and to give me a rank, I had to receive Soviet political training. The training was conducted by an officer of the NKVD.[8] We attended classes every day for about four weeks and were indoctrinated into communism. In addition to serving guard duty, I was also taught Russian, and my fluency greatly improved. When I completed the classes, I received the rank of lieutenant. All of this time no one ever knew that I was Jewish. I still called myself Jan Jerzowski.

As the Soviet Army recovered and began moving west, we always stayed about fifty or seventy kilometers behind the front lines. We were like an occupation force. The army brought the prisoners to us, and we did the translating for them. For about three months we stayed near Przemyśl while the front line reached my hometown of Krosno. In March of 1945 the Soviet front line had moved west of Kraków. At that time I took a leave and went back to Krosno to look for survivors.

CHAPTER 5

Surviving Inside the Camps

Recall that in September 1942, while Shlomo and Joshua remained in Krosno before the final liquidation of the Krosno ghetto, Michael and Moishe were sent to work with other Krosno tailors to make uniforms for the Ukrainian troops at an SS military camp at Moderówka. In this chapter Michael recounts his experiences in Moderówka and in concentration camps at Szebnie and in Auschwitz at Birkenau and Buna-Monowitz. Unlike the closed awareness context of the passing experience, where Jews had to hide their identity, camp life maintained an open awareness context where a person's Jewishness was acknowledged. In the camps Michael would not need to create the impression that he was a Christian Pole. Instead he would need to present an image of himself as someone who could perform productive labor and be of practical use to his captors.

MODERÓWKA

In Moderówka the Jewish barracks where the tailors worked and lived were separated from the rest of the camp in a compound that was surrounded with barbed wire and armed guards. Michael remembers that there were about thirty tailors, with two barracks for the male workers, a separate barrack for the female workers, and another barrack that was equipped with sewing machines and other equipment that had been confiscated from Jewish shops. But, as he notes:

Among all of the camps in which I was interned, Moderówka was the easiest to bear. We were given three meals a day from the same kitchen that the soldiers ate from. For a short while it looked like we might be able to hold out until the Soviets arrived. We heard through the grapevine that the German Army was in retreat and that we might soon be liberated. We had hope!

The guards at Moderówka occasionally took sport by slapping us around. The one time I recall most vividly was the night a Nazi officer came into our sleeping quarters and took out one man in his late twenties. Then he went into the women's quarters and took out one of our women. He took them both into an empty barrack, where he ordered them to strip and engage in lewd sexual acts, while the officer slashed them with a leather strap. After awhile he sent them back with a warning not to divulge what had happened. However, they told us anyway.

The Holocaust epiphany Michael remembers best at Moderówka involved an interrogation he endured after receiving a letter from Shlomo:

We were still able to receive some mail from the outside because the leader of our barrack had connections with the village postman. Previously my brothers and I had worked out a code so that we could communicate. In this code we referred to locations or other situations by names of people that we knew. After Shlomo fled Krosno, he wrote me a letter to let me know that he was alive and to give me the general location of his whereabouts. I destroyed the letter and envelope, although I worried that the Germans had already opened it and read it.

Two days later I was picked up by two Gestapo officers who knew me. (I had done some tailoring for them.) They took me to a concentration camp at Szebnie that was about seven kilometers from Moderówka. The two Gestapo officers also knew my brothers, and they wanted me to tell them where they were hiding out. I admitted that I had received a letter from Shlomo but that he had not said where he was. They asked me where the letter had been postmarked. I answered that I did not notice this. That earned me a good beating! During the interrogation they had a German shepherd dog lying on the floor, and they occasionally urged him to growl at me. After receiving another good beating, I managed to convince them that I knew nothing more. Obviously they knew where the letter had been mailed, but they could not find him. Shlomo in his wisdom had not mailed it from the city where he was staying. After about an hour of this ordeal, they called in a guard and told him to take me away. I did not know where he was taking me. I had visions that he was driving me into the forest to be shot. Instead he delivered me back to the barracks at Moderówka. Not many people survived Gestapo interrogations, so to this day I know somebody was watching over me.

Note Michael's reference here to "somebody . . . watching over me." Although he did not rely on religion to get him through critical junctures, he did experience times when the opportunity to exercise agency eluded him. Like Shlomo and other survivors, this remark implicitly acknowledges Michael's sense that his survival was in part contingent on luck or factors that he could not control. Moreover, he regrets Shlomo's decision to mail the letter. As he says, "I was happy to hear from my brother that he was alive, but at the same time I thought he should not have written because it could have cost me my life."

Some time after this episode, in August 1943, the Germans decided to close down the Moderówka tailor shop and deport the remaining Jews to another camp. But Michael hoped for a reprieve for Moishe and himself. As he recalls, "The SS camp commander liked having his own personal tailors, for he was just as greedy as the others, to make clothing for himself and his family that he shipped home to Germany. He received permission from the Gestapo to keep ten of the tailors for a while. The commander allowed the tailor who had been placed in charge of us, who was a cousin of mine, to choose who would stay.[1] I was sure that he would select Moishe and me. But to my great surprise, he did not."

SZEBNIE

Thus, Michael and Moishe were unable to avoid an undesirable status passage and were sent to the concentration camp at Szebnie, which was run by the SS.[2] Szebnie was located near the city of Rzeszów, about 130 kilometers southeast of Auschwitz. Michael remembers that

it was in Szebnie that I first experienced what a KZ, or *Katzett* [concentration camp], was really like. It was completely enclosed with towers manned by soldiers with machine guns and wire fences around the camp. There were about ten thousand prisoners. The barracks were furnished with bare wooden planks for sleeping. Meals were served to us whenever they felt like it — a small loaf of bread divided into twelve pieces and sometimes a little watery soup. The soup was derived from potatoes and turnips and occasionally some horse meat. It was extremely bitter. Now I knew what it meant to be hungry.

Szebnie had been a forced-labor camp, and Michael recalls working a few days, on and off, in a camp tailor shop. But mostly, he says, "they had us dig ditches, then cover them back up." He characterizes Szebnie primarily as a temporary holding facility where prisoners were kept before being sent to other labor camps or to death camps:

When the Germans liquidated a ghetto, they brought Jews there [Szebnie]. When it got overcrowded, they executed prisoners to make room for new arrivals. Nearby was a forest where they took people out of the camp and shot them. Then they took others out to help bury the dead. Of course, these people never returned either.

Occasionally a prisoner managed to escape on the way to the forest to be shot. When there was an escape, successful or not, the Germans practiced collective punishment and executed ten prisoners for each escapee. At these times all the prisoners, both men and women, were assembled in the center of the camp in a large field. We stood four deep, and an SS officer picked out at random whomever he pleased. The ten prisoners were then told to kneel, and the officer machine-gunned them all. He appeared to enjoy this.

I remember one time when they built ten crosses in the middle of the field. After all the prisoners were assembled, an SS officer picked out ten prisoners. Each prisoner was strapped to the cross, with his feet dangling above the ground. The rest of us had to stand at attention and watch the misery and listen to the cries of the condemned people. This lasted for many hours until all but one of them were dead. After the soldiers got tired, the camp commander announced through the loud-speaker that, because of his great compassion as a German officer, he would pardon the remaining living man. He ordered the rope holding the prisoner cut and then machine-gunned him to death.

For more minor infractions of camp rules the SS would order twenty-five lashes. The guards would put your head into this contraption and begin beating you. The inmate would have to count out the lashes, and if he lost count, the guards started over again. Most people could not survive this type of beating.

One morning my brother Moishe was taken away with a large group of prisoners. That was the last I ever saw of him. I didn't even have a chance to say good-bye to him. After the war I met some survivors from Rzeszów who knew him and said they had seen him being killed by the Germans.

Auschwitz: Birkenau

In the early part of November 1943 the liquidation of the Szebnie camp forced Michael to endure yet another Holocaust epiphany. At this time most of the prisoners were either taken to the forest to be shot or transported to Auschwitz.[3] According to Michael:

All the prisoners were assembled and led out of the camp. On each side of the road soldiers armed with rifles were stationed, ready to shoot. We were ordered to run. We were sure we were being taken to the forest to be shot. I remember joining with others all around me in praying loudly and reciting, "Sh'ma Yisrael," "Oh hear me, God." At that time there was nobody else to turn to. The only place to turn was to God. Instead we ended up at the train depot, where we saw huge piles of clothing. We were ordered to undress. It was a cold, rainy day, and I had only my shorts on. We were forced to get into standing-room-only cattle cars. When all the cars were filled, the doors were locked from the outside and the train departed.

The journey lasted about two days, and not once were the doors opened. We were all squeezed together so tight that some of us even suffocated. We were not given any food or water, and we had to urinate right where we were standing. We were not even given a bucket. Many people died before we arrived at our destination. When the train finally came to a stop, the doors were opened and we were ordered out. We had arrived at Birkenau.

Birkenau was adjacent to the first Auschwitz concentration camp (Auschwitz I), which was located about sixty kilometers west of Kraków. Birkenau (Auschwitz II) was part of a larger group of camps that consisted of more than forty subcamps, including Buna-Monowitz (Auschwitz III).[4] It was the largest Nazi concentration

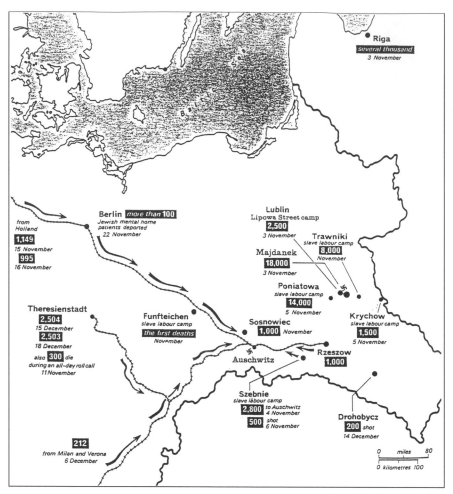

Deportations and mass shootings, November–December 1943. Copyright © Martin Gilbert, *Atlas of the Holocaust* (2nd ed.), William Morrow, New York, 1993.

camp in which Jews were exterminated by means of poison gas and burned in huge crematoria.

On first arrival at Auschwitz, many prisoners failed to comprehend the significance of the "selection" procedure that they immediately faced.[5] Others, like Michael, were quick to realize what was happening and took action to maximize their chances of surviving this "crucial moment." As Michael recalls:

Upon our arrival we were surrounded by SS soldiers and ordered to line up in formation four deep. Then the segregation or selection process began. Women and children were separated from the men. A couple of officers went through the lines and pointed a finger at each prisoner and ordered, "Step left, step right, left, right." I'm quite certain Dr. Josef Mengele was one of them. I quickly surmised that one group was probably going to be killed and that the other group might be saved to perform slave labor. I closely observed which group appeared to have a better chance of survival and assumed that the group with the stronger and taller people would be picked for work and that the group with the weaker people would be killed. I was standing next to a middle-aged man who had an obviously crippled leg. When he was ordered to the left, I knew that this was not the group I wanted to be in. So when I was ordered left, I went right. The whole selection process, which took about an hour, occurred with such speed that the guards did not notice that I had disobeyed the order and switched groups. I assume that others did the same thing, but I didn't see it myself. You had to have nerve to do what I did, but I didn't hesitate.

After the selection was completed, the two groups were assembled and separated. Several trucks arrived, and all the people standing in the group to my left were ordered to board. I had a young friend, Herman Levine,[6] whom I had met at Moderówka and who had arrived with me at Birkenau. He was on the truck and realized that he was in danger. When his truck took off, he jumped down and ran over to my group. He was lucky that no one saw him, for the several thousand people who left on those trucks were never seen or heard from again. Later we learned that they were all gassed in phony shower rooms and incinerated in the crematoria.

Our group was ordered to march. I was barefooted and had only my shorts on. It was a very cold and rainy night, and we had nothing to eat or drink for many hours. We were marched into a large compound where the showers were located. We were ordered to strip, and some camp workers shaved our heads. We were then ordered into the freezing cold showers and to line up alphabetically for further processing. I tried not to be separated from another friend of mine who had been with me since Moderówka and Szebnie. His name was Joel Turek. He told the SS that his last name was Boigen so that we could be closer in line. Once in line each prisoner was registered and tattooed with a number on his left arm. I was given number 160914. Turek was given number 160915. I was referred to by this number during the whole time I was incarcerated. I no longer had a name. When number 160914 was called, I responded.

After being tattooed, we were given a pair of striped pants, shirt, and jacket, all of thin summer weight that did not protect you from the wind and the cold. We were also issued a cap and uncomfortable wooden clogs for shoes. We were assigned to various barracks and indoctrinated into the prevailing rules of the camp. Finally we were given a bowl of soup, which was the first food we had been given since leaving Szebnie.

After this account of his first selection and his introduction to Birkenau, Michael goes on to describe the organization of the camp:

The Auschwitz concentration camps, including Birkenau, were run with German precision and efficiency. The SS designated a chain of command and, unlike Szebnie, appointed prisoners to be in charge of the day-to-day operations. A prisoner known as the *Lager Führer* or *Lagerältester* was in charge of the entire camp. He appointed *Blockälteste* as block or barrack leaders and *Kapos* as trustees or leaders of the work *Kommandos*. There were also different types of inmates at Birkenau. Prisoners with a criminal record were identified with green triangles of cloth sewn on the front of their uniforms. Prisoners incarcerated for political crimes were identified with a red triangle of cloth. Jewish inmates were classed as political prisoners and identified with a red-and-yellow Jewish star. Although the majority of prisoners were Jews, there were many who were not.

The inmates of Birkenau were housed in army-type barracks and made to sleep in bunk beds that consisted of bare wooden platforms with a little straw. The bunks were three high, and we could barely sit up in them. With as many as ten of us sleeping on each platform, we felt like sardines. The Blockältester of each barrack chose two or three other prisoners to assist him. He had enormous power over the inmates of the barrack. He distributed the food rations and kept order in the barrack. Rules were strict, and you were best to abide by them, for he could beat you to death.

Michael notes that it did not take long for the prisoners to become aware of the gas chambers and crematoria because of the smell and smoke that were coming from the tall chimneys in the camp:

Main concentration camps in Nazi-occupied Europe. Reprinted with permission of Macmillan Publishing Company from *Encyclopedia of the Holocaust*, vol. 1, Israel Gutman, Editor in Chief. Copyright © by Macmillan Publishing Company.

If you didn't realize this on your own, a veteran prisoner or a guard would sometimes say, "See that smoke up there? That's where you'll be going anytime." The crematoria were serviced by a special group of prisoners called *Sonderkommandos* whose job was to sort out the possessions of the dead and dispose of the bodies. Usable clothing and shoes were stockpiled in warehouses [*Kanada*] and shipped to Germany. Another group of inmates pulled the gold out from the mouths of the dead. Some of the gold was directly shipped to Germany, but much was diverted from shipment by the guards, who would have inmate craftsmen melt the gold and make precision pieces of jewelry. These valuable items were then sent home to wives and families. The guards and officers saw no reason not to enrich themselves since there was plenty to go around and the Third Reich would not miss it as long as they did not know about it.

There was a constant flow of new arrivals to the camp. In some instances transports would come and most of the people were sent directly to the gas chambers. At other times a larger proportion would be designated for work. It all depended on the Germans' need for forced labor and the room available in the barracks.

Every morning at 5:00 A.M. a bell rang and all inmates were ordered out of the barracks. We were given ten minutes to use the latrines, and after receiving some coffee or ersatz [a coffee substitute], we had to assemble by the barracks for a roll call or body count, which was supervised by an SS officer. After the body count we were assigned to various work Kommandos inside the perimeter of the camp. I have heard that some inmates at Birkenau worked outside the camps, but I did not.[7]

When I was in Birkenau, we didn't perform any productive work, but the SS gave us nonproductive assignments. Mostly we carried heavy stones from one side of the camp to the other and then reversed the procedure. We were followed by SS guards armed with rifles and German shepherd dogs. At a command from the dog handler, the dogs would bite or just scare you. The guards often did this just for fun and sport, and they would beat us with their rifles or wooden boards. This work could go on for hours at a time, and when the guards got tired, they would leave us standing in front of the barracks for the rest of the day. We did everything we could just to keep from freezing, including exercising or just huddling together to benefit from each other's body heat. It was pure misery! Sometimes they even made us remain in a crouched position. Midday they gave us some watery soup, but we were not allowed inside the barracks until after the evening body count, which occurred at about 5:00 P.M. Following the body count we went into the barracks and received our meager ration of soup. We may have been given some bread as well, but I don't remember this. By 9:00 P.M. the lights were turned out, and everyone had to be in their bunk. The next morning we went through the same routine again.

AUSCHWITZ: BUNA-MONOWITZ

Michael spent about four weeks under these circumstances in Birkenau. Then one morning a selection took place after the body count. Michael recalls, "Several thousand inmates — including me and my friends, Herman and Turek — were picked and under armed guards marched to another camp about seven kilometers away. This new establishment was called Buna-Monowitz [Auschwitz III]. When we arrived, they had us checked by prisoners who were supposed to be dentists, but I don't think they were. Their job was to remove any gold in the inmates' mouths. In addition, if you had any bad teeth, they immediately pulled them out. It was there that I had my two gold crowns removed."

According to Michael Unger, prisoners "who had lived in a more or less normal environment immediately before arriving" at Auschwitz had a more difficult time overcoming their initial shock and trauma, especially if this was the first time they had to cope with the sudden loss of family. Others, like Michael, had been more gradually acclimated to the concentration camp experience, to the extent this was possible, and "continued to ponder ways of ameliorating their situation."[8] Michael estimates that he could not have survived Birkenau for more than three months but remembers that "it was immediately clear that Buna was an improvement over Birkenau. The barracks were neat and clean, and the bunk beds were covered with straw. Unlike Birkenau, only two inmates were assigned to each bunk. On first impression I felt that survival was possible here. I could see that, while some inmates looked emaciated, others seemed well fed. I assumed that some prisoners were managing to get additional resources, and I knew that I would have to find out where these resources came from if I was to survive."

In Erving Goffman's terms, Michael had already surmised that behind the "primary adjustments" to camp life were the "secondary adjustments" that some inmates had made to circumvent their captors' "assumptions as to what [they] should do and get and hence what [they] should be. . . . Every organization . . . involves a discipline of activity, . . . an obligation to be of a given character and to dwell in a given world. . . . Secondary adjustments represent ways in which the individual stands apart from the role and the self that were taken for granted for him by the institution."[9] In the camps a person's life depended on making these secondary adjustments. Inmates "conformed because otherwise they died," but they also innovated because "otherwise they died."[10]

An inmate's position in the work process of the camp was the most important factor in determining life chances at Auschwitz, and survival depended on each inmate's ongoing appraisal about which work groups were best or least dangerous.[11] Kommandos that did not require hard physical labor and that allowed a person to remain inside, sheltered from the cold, were the most desirable. As Michael observes:

> Some work Kommandos were extremely hard, making it unlikely a prisoner could survive for more than three months. Other Kommandos were easier, enabling one to go on for years. Unlike Birkenau, Buna was a camp where important work was being performed for the Third Reich by IG Farben Industries. IG Farben was the largest chemical company in Germany, and it manufactured various kinds of war and building materials.[12] They paid the SS for the labor done by the prisoners, who, of course, did not receive payment in return. Prisoners, especially those with skills, were valued as long as they were strong enough to perform productive work. IG Farben needed tool-and-die makers, carpenters, chemists, and the like, and they were even willing to train some of the younger people for the skilled jobs.

Michael regrets missing an opportunity for an easier work assignment when he first arrived at Buna:

> I had a painful sore on the insole of my foot from the constant rubbing of my shoes. So after we were assigned to our barracks, I walked over to the Ka-Be [Krankenbau, or camp hospital]. In my absence the Kapos asked inmates what types of trades they were in and began assigning people to different work Kommandos. At the Ka-Be they applied ointment and bandaged my foot. When I returned from the hospital two or three hours later, all the special assignments were taken, and I was put into the category of a simple laborer. I was immediately separated from my friends and put in a different barrack, for Turek had managed to get assigned for training in tool-and-die making and Herman in carpentry.

Michael remembers Buna as being well organized and as operating on the same principle as the other camps, with Blockälteste and Kapos in charge:

The morning ritual was similar to what I experienced in Birkenau — getting up at 5:00 A.M., ten minutes for using the latrine, and a cup of coffee. Then we were assembled for a body count in the center of the camp on a large terrace [the *Appellplatz*] that held all the inmates. Afterwards the inmates were separated into various Kommandos and marched out of the camp. As we approached the gates, I saw a large sign over the gates saying, "*Arbeit Macht Frei*," meaning "Work Makes One Free." An orchestra consisting of inmate musicians played as we marched through the gates. It was like a military parade. The Kapo saluted the SS guards, and the inmates removed their caps to show their respect to the guards.

The Kapo in charge of each Kommando was responsible to the Germans to complete all designated work. He had the authority to administer punishment to the prisoners under his command. It was important to have a good Kapo. A good Kapo would not hit you to show his authority unless he was being observed by the SS guards. Some Kapos managed to remain decent human beings and help others if they could. But a bad Kapo could be extremely brutal and sadistic. Often the SS chose people for these very characteristics. Many were murderers or other criminals under long-term sentences who were transferred from civilian prisons. Kapos could be gentiles or Jews and were of all nationalities. There were even some Jews, who were decent people before the war, who turned out to be mean Kapos because the only way they knew how to survive was to identify with the system. Indeed, there were Jewish prisoners who used the same language on me and other Jews as the Germans, calling me a "Goddamn dirty Jew, a shyster." Some of these men had already been incarcerated for four or five years. And after surviving much brutality themselves, and finally arriving at a position of authority, they changed psychologically.[13] To be sure, not everyone was like this, but a large number were. They would stand with the SS guards laughing as they watched the rest of us toiling at hard labor. In addition, we continuously appraised the different SS guards. Was he going to take pleasure in abusing us? We had nicknames for all of them, like Ivan the Terrible and Fritz the Butcher. But there were some who would leave you alone if you just did your work and stayed orderly. They had their own troubles and were worried about being sent to the Russian front or being captured by the Soviets.

The Kommando to which I was first assigned was marched under armed guard through muddy terrain about two kilometers out of the camp to a large area of completely deserted land. When we arrived, we began digging ditches, in preparation for what I don't know. We loaded lorries with dirt and pushed the cars on rails to another place to dump the dirt. It was hard work and it was cold and rainy. And we received many beatings. Our Kapos were merciless because they wanted to show the SS guards how tough they could be. We worked till noon, when we got a half-hour break. We were allowed to sit in a little shack that had an oven stove, which the guards sat around to warm themselves. We were given some soup and then put back to work.

At about 4:00 P.M. we were marched back into camp. When we returned, the orchestra played, and as tired as we were, we had to march into the camp like soldiers. By 5:00 P.M. all the Kommandos were assembled for another body count. All accounted for, we were dismissed and returned to the barracks. Each inmate received a bowl of soup and about six ounces of bread. After a hard long day of work, the ration of food was hardly enough. I was still hungry. Every night after we ate, we were also inspected for lice by one of the trustees in the barrack. If lice were found, we were sent to a public bathhouse, where they sprayed you all night with a hose of cold water. Twice I was sent to that bathhouse. It was a horrible experience, and I did not sleep the entire night. Otherwise we were allowed to linger around the barracks until about 9:00 P.M., when the lights were put out and we got into our bunks.

In his early days at Buna Michael did not have a steady Kommando and was repeatedly assigned from one Kommando to another. He remembers that

I did a lot of digging and learned how to throw dirt with a shovel pretty far. Because if you didn't learn, you got a lot of beatings. Once I was assigned to unload coal from a train. I got black like a coal miner, and there was no way to wash yourself clean. Eventually I was sent to the huge IG Farben industrial complex that was about two kilometers from the camp, where they were manufacturing cement blocks. I worked outside and loaded sacks of cement into a cement mixer that was operated by two inmates. A single line of inmates was formed, and each of us had to pick up a sack weighing about one hundred pounds, carry it over to the cement mixer, and unload it. Then we had to go back to the pile for another sack. We had to work fast, and if you didn't, you would get kicked by the Kapo. After awhile I was reassigned to work on the actual manufacturing of the blocks. This process involved assembling the forms into which the cement was poured.

After the cement was poured and hardened, the forms were removed and the bricks loaded into lorries. When the lorries were fully loaded, three workers pushed them to another area for shipment.

This went on for several weeks, and I was getting hungrier and weaker by the day. I dreamed of having an extra ration of food but hadn't figured out how to get it. I had learned that there were two classes of inmates — those who existed only on food rations allocated to them by the camp authorities and those who managed to supplement their rations with extra contraband food. These inmates were referred to as "organizers." An organizer was a person who was successful at finding ways of acquiring additional provisions. On the other hand, prisoners who were unable to organize continued to deteriorate. Those who lost a lot of weight and became emaciated were known as Muselmänner. A Muselmann's days were limited. He either died of malnutrition or beatings (because he couldn't work) or was sent to the gas chambers after a selection.

At great risk of getting caught and beaten by the Kapos or the SS guards, there were many ways an enterprising or opportunistic inmate could organize in the camps. For instance, some inmates were able to get extra rations by performing personal services, like tailoring for prominent inmates like Blockälteste, Kapos, or kitchen personnel. Some of the younger inmates performed sexual favors. I myself never encountered any advances, but it was a known fact that many Blockälteste had their favorite boy, whom they sheltered, fed, and protected in exchange for sexual favors. This was true of my friend Herman, who was two or three years younger than me.

In addition, some of the [non-Jewish] Polish inmates were even allowed to receive food packages from their relatives. Some inmates, especially Kapos, were in a position to barter with the civilian employees who worked at the IG Farben plant. These civilians were interested in the various commodities that were being stored in the warehouses but that were not available on the open market. In return, civilians gave inmates food — a loaf of bread, a pound of salami or pork meat, or some butter. Since the inmate then had plenty to eat, he was no longer dependent on his camp rations and could give them to any inmate he favored. A Kapo in this position would share the food with his favorite underlings. In this way an inmate who was successful as an organizer, or who established a good relationship with a Kapo or other organizers, had enough food to sustain himself in good health. He was able to perform better on the job and avoid further beatings and being selected to go to the gas chambers.

LIVERPOOL JOHN MOORES UNIVERSITY
LEARNING SERVICES

To organize, an inmate had to establish himself in the network of camp relationships that controlled access to resources. Up to this point Michael was having great difficulty finding a way to do this. As he recalls:

Whenever it was possible, we tried to form friendships to support and help each other. This was much more difficult in Birkenau than in Buna. However, we were reluctant to form attachments because we could be separated the next day. It was very traumatic if you had a friend and all of a sudden you were separated. I had only brief contact with my friends Turek and Herman after we had been separated. They were in better Kommandos and had more opportunities to organize. Turek, however, never offered me any extra food. I asked him for help, but he kept telling me that he didn't have anything. Yet I could see that neither he nor anyone else in his barrack were undernourished. Herman, on the other hand, did give me some food. In fact, he offered it to me; I didn't even have to ask him for it. In addition to being the homosexual lover of one of the influential Kapos in the camp, he was also in one of the better Kommandos. Thus, he had plenty of food at his disposal.

While Michael was working in the cement Kommando, a car rolled back and hit him on his right shin. Within minutes his leg swelled up to almost twice its size, and by the end of the day he could no longer walk. He remembers being carried by other prisoners back to the camp and then being admitted to the camp hospital:

The hospital was staffed with inmate doctors, nurses, and orderlies. The chief doctor was a Pole. The secretary and record keeper was a Polish Jew. The doctor performed emergency surgery on my leg. I was given chloroform, and two incisions were made to drain out the puss to prevent the spread of infection. When I awoke, I found myself on a bunk, my leg bandaged, and in a lot of pain. I was not given anything to ease the pain. On my fifth day in the hospital an orderly advised me to ask to be discharged. He hinted that the SS doctor inspected the hospital records, and when he saw that a patient was not discharged for a week and put back to work, he would send him to Birkenau to be gassed. Thus, I asked to be discharged and left the hospital with my leg wrapped in paper bandages. I was told to come back in the evenings after work to change the bandages.

I was reassigned to a different barrack and a different Kommando. The majority of inmates in my new Kommando were Poles who were receiving food packages from relatives. Having extra food, their health was better than most of the Jews in the group, and they were able to perform better at work. The work was in construction and was very hard. It was winter and very cold, and we worked outside all day. After several weeks I began to look like a Muselmann. One Sunday morning there was a selection. All inmates stood naked, and the SS doctor, who, I believe, was Dr. Koening, inspected us. He picked out about one-third of the inmates, and his assistant recorded their numbers as unfit for work. They were all Jews since the Poles still looked healthy. The following morning after a body count was conducted and the Kommandos were assembled, the numbers of the prisoners selected the previous day were called, and they were taken into a large holding room. I was among them. After several hundred of us were assembled, the same SS doctor came in for a second look. He reconsidered and released a few, who were sent back to the barracks. I knew that for me the end was near. I had no illusions about the promises of being sent to a resort camp. There was nothing I could do but wait. Yet I hoped for a miracle, and indeed a miracle did happen.

This was a "crucial moment" epiphany of Michael's survival, and his reference to a miracle or luck in getting him through is noteworthy. However, his survival was significantly dependent on his taking the initiative to seek opportunities and, once again, on his ability to exchange his resource as a tailor to advance his position. Important as well was the support he received from other, more privileged, inmates who were in a position to make decisions about saving lives and who appeared to operate on the basis of a utilitarian ethic. Although these inmates recognized that individual "lives would end," they hoped that some would "have the strength to continue."[14] As Michael explains:

I was lingering around near the entrance of the room. The chief doctor who had operated on my leg came in with his assistant, the record keeper. They spoke Polish to each other, and I heard the doctor tell his assistant to pick out several youngsters. I presented myself before them and asked them to help me. The assistant grabbed my arm, marked off my tattoo number, and sent me off to the barracks. He did the same to a few others who were under twenty years of age. Later I found out what their motives were. Since they had patients in the hospital who were doomed because of age and bad health, they substituted us for those unfortunate patients, thus living up to an unwritten code of saving the younger people.

When I returned to the barracks, only the Blockältester was there since the other inmates had not yet returned from work. He was a German Jew who greeted me with sarcasm and skepticism. He told me that I had only postponed my transport and that I would be picked in the next selection.[15]

All day I was thinking that I had to find a way to be assigned to a better Kommando, for surely I had no chance of surviving if I had to continue with all the hard work under the same conditions. I went back to the hospital to see the record keeper. I thanked him for saving my life but told him it would be a useless gesture if I had to continue in the same Kommando. I asked him if he could please use his influence to arrange for me to be placed in a better Kommando. Again I lucked out. He gave me a letter to the person in charge of work assignments [the Arbeitsdienst], who assigned me to Kommando 1 and to a change of barracks.

Membership in Kommando 1 was a desirable status passage that moved Michael into a different part of the camp social structure. As he says:

Kommando 1 was one of the best in the camp. One had to be lucky to be in this Kommando. When I marched out to work with this Kommando, I was optimistic. We went to a warehouse that had all kinds of electrical supplies. For the first time in many months I was inside a heated building and safe from the outside elements. The Kapo assigned me to sort and clean electrical lightbulbs. The work was so easy and boring that I had trouble staying awake. Once the Kapo caught me dozing off, and he slapped me and gave me a warning to look busy.

The Kapo of Kommando 1 was an eastern German by the name of Hans who spoke both German and Polish. He was a large, powerful man and had a green triangle on his uniform. He had been a prisoner in Germany, where he had been serving a life sentence for murder. I had seen this Kapo enraged. He could beat an inmate half to death, so I was happy I got off easy.

Still, I was not able to organize, and I was constantly hungry. Then I got lucky. I noticed that the Kapo was missing a couple of buttons from his tailored uniform, so I offered to sew them on for him. I told him that I was a tailor by profession. He was pleased and asked if I knew how to sew pants. I responded that if he got me material, I could do it. When we returned to camp that evening, he had obtained several long striped overcoats of heavy winter material for me to use to make a pair of trousers for him. He gave me needles, thread, and a pair of scissors. He had the machine shop make a thimble for me from a half-inch pipe, and I was all set. There was a little room in the warehouse that he designated to me as a workshop, a cement bomb shelter that was off limits to the other inmates.

It took me two weeks to finish the trousers, and he was very pleased. He told me from now on I was to be his personal valet. I was to wash his laundry and iron his clothes. In return I would receive his camp food rations, for he had no need for ordinary camp food. He assigned me to one of the first three bunks in the barracks, which were reserved for the elite. It even had a quilt. He issued me a new uniform and told me that I had to keep myself neat and clean, wash my shirt (which I laid out to dry at night), and take daily showers in the communal washrooms with soap that he provided for me.

I was now on the way to becoming an organizer, and I began to have hope. Receiving my Kapo's food rations in addition to my own, I started to gain weight and feel much stronger. Three times a week I reported to the hospital to change my bandages, and although my leg was still painful, it began to heal. Every evening I showered with cold water because hot water was not provided. But I forced myself to endure it. Previously I had not seen the point of showering without soap because you couldn't get clean and in the winter you would just expose yourself to getting pneumonia. But now as a privileged person I had to think differently. Because if you looked dirty, you would get more beatings. If you made a better impression, a guard or another Kapo would think that you were someone to respect, that you had something going for you, some connections.

Soon the Kapo introduced me to the organizing scheme. On a few occasions I put small electrical motors or other supplies into a wheel-barrow, covered it with trash, and dumped it outside in a designated place. From there another inmate in the service of our Kapo loaded them [motors or supplies] onto a pickup truck used by a civilian, who kept them for his personal use or, more likely, sold them on the black market to another civilian. In another instance a civilian truck driver would come to the warehouse with a withdrawal order for certain supplies from the warehouse that were to be delivered to other subsidiaries. If his withdrawal order called for six electrical motors, seven might be put on the truck. In return, the civilian gave us food. Being a party to the scheme, I occasionally received some of this food. When the next selection occurred and the SS doctor was picking out Muselmän-ner, I was bypassed. I was fit to work and no longer in danger of the selections.

Although he now had sufficient food, Michael was reluctant to give any away. He remembers only one instance in which he gave a Polish Jew in need some soup, bread, and tobacco. "Mostly I con-sumed all the food I had right on the spot. I never rationed my food because I felt that if I tried to save it, someone might steal it. Although there was an unwritten code against stealing from other inmates, people would do it if given the chance. So I would just eat all that I had. I figured even if I didn't get anymore for twenty-four hours, I was filled up and wasn't hungry."

It might be tempting to be judgmental and ask why Michael was not more willing to sacrifice some of his provisions for the benefit of others. But although an inmate was dependent on others for survival, it would be a mistake to assume that only acts of solidarity helped individuals stay alive.[16] A prisoner who applied altruistic moral stan-dards in an absolute way inevitably perished. Michael never stole anything from another inmate, but his decision to focus on his own basic needs appears to have been an important factor in his personal survival. As he explains, "For the most part Auschwitz was a situa-tion of 'every man for himself.' I thought about myself, not about other people's needs." Perhaps Lawrence Langer's distinction between acts that are "selfish" and acts that are "self-ish" best describes the dilemma: "The selfish act ignores the needs of others through choice when the agent is in a position to help without injur-ing one's self in any appreciable way. Selfishness is motivated by greed, indifference, malice, and many value-laden categories. . . . [With] the self-ish act, however, . . . [one] is vividly aware of the needs of others but because of the nature of the situation is unable to choose freely the generous impulse that a more compassionate nature yearns to express."[17]

However, there was a time after Michael had already become an organizer when he remembers coming to the defense of some of the less influential inmates:

I was sent out with some others to unload and move some heavy office furniture that was packed in crates. The assistant Kapo who was in charge was mean and started abusing some of the boys. He left me alone because he knew I was favored by my Kapo. But I finally got so angry with him that I interfered. I said, "Why don't you leave these fellows alone?" He raised his stick at me, and I grabbed it from him. I obviously felt protected, for otherwise I never would have done this. He put me on report to my Kapo, who later called me aside. He told me, "Now don't you do that anymore. I can't allow you to challenge the man who is in charge. I'm going to let you go this time, but I warn you not to do it again."

Although Michael's personal position was now fairly secure, survival in Buna was by no means assured. He recognizes that a considerable amount of luck was necessary to survive. As he says, "Diarrhea was one of the biggest killers, and I was lucky I didn't get too sick. I had diarrhea several times — it was running down by legs — but I managed to get through it."

Michael also feared being punished for violations of camp rules. He recalls:

Any infraction of the rules resulted in an inmate receiving twenty-five lashes on his behind in full view of the whole camp population. Occasionally the body count was not accurate, or some prisoners would collapse or die someplace on the camp premises. A search was made and all of us had to stand for many hours at attention until they were found, no matter what the weather conditions were. All prisoners had to be accounted for before we were allowed back to the barracks.

Every once in awhile there were escape attempts, but most of the escaped prisoners were caught. They were returned and sentenced to be hanged. At these times several scaffolds were erected on the terrace after the body count. Then all inmates stood at attention and were forced to watch the hanging. One time I witnessed the bravest act by several of the condemned prisoners who were members of the camp resistance movement. They walked up the scaffold with their heads up and proud expressions on their faces. When the SS officer pronounced the sentence and the hangmen put the rope around their necks, each condemned man yelled out [in German] in a clear loud voice, "We are the last ones!" Another yelled, "You are losing the war and will surely pay for it!" And then they were hanged.

The opportunities to escape or in other ways resist were quite limited. Many of us were aware of the Germans' practice of collective punishment even before we got to the camps.[18] If I, for example, would have decided to attack a German and thus risk my own death, I would have been a party to the execution of my family, friends, and neighbors. So even in the camps, we were not necessarily favorably inclined toward resisters. We did sympathize with the more skilled and experienced prisoners who were planning organized escapes or sabotage efforts that were more likely to be successful, but most of us were not privy to these schemes.[19] They were very secretive, and I was never in a position to join them. But I don't think I would have joined them if I could have because I felt that my chances of survival in Buna were greater if I didn't risk being executed for something I could choose to avoid. Others, however, may have felt that they would be killed anyway, which could have happened without notice at any time.

Michael remembers two or three times when the International Red Cross actually came to inspect Buna. "On these occasions the camp was cleaned up and we were given better food — a piece of cheese or salami. Cigarettes were even issued. The camp was made up to look like a regular military camp. No one would tell the Red Cross representatives what was really going on for fear of what would happen when they left."

Nevertheless, the Allied bombings, which began in the summer of 1944, were a source of hope for Michael and the other inmates. According to Michael:

The Allies began to bomb the IG Farben work complex because it was producing materials for the war effort. The planes could come at any time of the day. I believe the British came in the day and the Americans at night. The prisoners enjoyed this in spite of the danger it posed to us. Some of the inmates were, in fact, killed, and I could have been easily killed as well. But I thought, what was there to lose? It was the greatest pleasure to see the planes coming in! It was a sign of hope! It gave me an extra psychological boost to get through the next day because I felt that every additional day I survived I was that much closer to being liberated.

After the first bombing we were immediately ordered to dig ditches around almost every one of the buildings. When the planes approached, an air alert was sounded. Sirens screamed, and everyone, including the SS guards, jumped into the ditches. Even without a direct hit, you could feel the earth shake, and we thought that the ground would collapse in on us. The guards were just as scared as we were. The difference was that, while we were hopeful, they were in fear that it was the beginning of the end for them. The pity of it was that the Allies chose not to bomb Birkenau. They were only concerned about their own war needs, not about saving the lives of thousands of people who could not have been killed and disposed of in such large numbers without the gas chambers and crematoria. This is my main criticism of the way the Allies conducted themselves during the war.[20]

CHAPTER 6

The End of the War and Liberation

In the final portion of their account Michael and Shlomo relate their experiences toward the end of the war and the immediate aftermath of their liberation. Michael begins with his recollection of his final days at Auschwitz and the travails of the infamous Death March. Then Shlomo picks up the story of what transpired after he took leave from the Soviet Army.

EVACUATION FROM AUSCHWITZ: THE DEATH MARCH

Michael's remaining days at Auschwitz were filled with the hope of continuing Allied advancement. Yet this phase of the war was only the beginning of the end for him — the beginning of a torturous retreat into Germany. According to Michael:

Some inmates were able to get information about the progress of the war through contacts with civilians or the SS guards. This information was passed on through the grapevine. While I was in Buna, we knew just how far the Soviets had advanced on the eastern front. And this is what kept us alive, what gave me the will to hold on — the hope that we would be liberated by the Red Army.

By January of 1945 we could hear the sound of Soviet artillery, for the Red Army was only about twenty to thirty kilometers away. We hoped to be liberated immediately, but this did not happen. The Germans feared falling into the hands of the Soviets, and they decided to retreat. All of the prisoners were assembled and prepared to march on foot back into Germany. There was chaos in the camp. I did not know it at the time, but the guards were in such a hurry to leave that they did not search the camp for those prisoners who did not report to the appropriate place. Instead these prisoners hid out in the latrines or wherever they could. I thought about doing this myself, but I was afraid to take the risk of being discovered and possibly being shot.[1]

About ten days later the 650 prisoners who remained at Buna were liberated by the Soviets.[2] However, more than one-third of the more than 700,000 inmates recorded as having been in various Nazi concentration camps in January 1945 lost their lives during the subsequent evacuation effort, which has come to be known as the Death Marches.[3] In retrospect, Michael regrets his decision not to hide because, as he says, "the following months were the most difficult I had to endure during my entire ordeal," an undesirable status passage that allowed even fewer chances for purposeful action than the camp:

> We first marched for over two days and nights to a camp in the city of Gliwice. We must have walked over fifty kilometers, stopping only when the guards wanted to rest. The roads were covered with snow, and it was very cold. Guards were posted every fifty or hundred feet, and any prisoner who tripped or fell behind was immediately shot and left dead on the road. Many of the prisoners met this fate. It took all my strength and determination to keep up. Most of the prisoners were wearing shoes with wooden bottoms. The snow would stick and pile up under these shoes. It was like walking on stilts, and every fifty feet or so they had to kick the snow off, or they couldn't walk. I was lucky that I was one of the privileged inmates at the time who was wearing leather shoes, which had been taken away from people who had been gassed. They were not a matching pair, but it did make it easier for me to walk. There was no food distributed on the march. Fortunately I had from Buna a loaf of bread that I hid under my shirt and nibbled on throughout the march.
>
> When we finally arrived at Gliwice, we entered the camp hoping to get some food and rest. Instead it was a nightmare. The camp was already overcrowded. There was hardly any food available and only standing room in the barracks. We were tired and exhausted. I found shelter in a shed where some prisoners slept. We huddled together for warmth. At daylight I woke up to find that many of them were dead. I

don't know how many were already dead before I got there and how many had died during the night.

The next morning we were assembled and marched to a train depot. We were loaded onto open cattle cars, packed like sardines. The train left the station with snow falling on us. I found a spot near the wall, away from the center of the car. Those who dared to sit down were promptly sat upon and died of suffocation. The dead were thrown overboard.

Although Michael had opportunities to attempt escape, he did not feel that the risk was worth taking. In this case, as in his decision not to remain at Auschwitz, Michael exercised his agency by not acting. As he recalls:

Some prisoners took their chances and jumped overboard. The guards shot at them from the moving train, killing most of them while the train kept going. My friend Herman urged me to jump with him, but I hesitated. I felt that he was stronger than me and that I wouldn't be able to make it. Maybe he was braver and had more courage. We said our good-byes, and with several others he jumped. Although it was night, the white snow made it look like daylight. The guards fired several shots at them. I was sure that they were hit, but after the war I met Herman in Munich. He said that a couple of the men who had jumped with him had been killed but that the rest had escaped into the surrounding fields. They hid out for about a week until they were liberated by the Soviet troops. Herman eventually emigrated to Canada.

While Herman was liberated, my ordeal got worse. The train continued west. I lost my sense of time, but it must have taken five or seven days until we reached our destination. All that time we had nothing to eat or drink except snow. We arrived in Oranienburg on the outskirts of Berlin, the capital of Germany. We were taken to a large hall with room for several hundred people. There was straw on the floor for sleeping. It was obvious that this was a temporary holding place and that many prisoners had passed through here. We were given some soup and allowed to sleep. Among the prisoners I recognized Fred Seiden, a distant relative of mine. It was an unbelievable reunion, and we were elated to have found each other! He told me that his wife and child were killed by the Germans in Poland before he was arrested and sent to a concentration camp. We were separated from each other several days later but were reunited in Germany after the war. Later Fred emigrated to Chicago.

From Oranienburg I was put on a train and transported to a concentration camp in Flossenbürg. The camp was located on high terrain surrounded by forests. It was very overcrowded with new arrivals like me who had been brought there from other camps that had been evacuated because of the advancing Soviet Army. We were a mixture of many nationalities; you could hear a variety of languages — German, Polish, French, Greek, Russian, and others. The temperature was always below zero, and we were not allowed into the barracks until night. All day we just stood around in the cold. The food rations were meager. There was no work to be done except to sweep the compound or carry the dead bodies to the outdoor brick fireplaces. And there were many dead. One time I was grabbed by a *Kapo* to help pick up dead people and shove them into the ovens. I did this for several hours until I managed to escape at the first opportunity.

I remember one morning when I woke up and saw some bread lying next to a *Muselmann*. I shook him and discovered that he was dead. I took the bread and ate it up in a hurry. Normally we were fed once a day. But one day they gave us the next day's ration a day in advance. We lined up and received a bowl of soup and a slice of bread. I carried the soup in one hand and the bread in the other. I walked into the barracks to my bunk to eat when suddenly a hand from the outside grabbed my bread through an open window. I put down the bowl of soup to chase the thief, who was a Russian prisoner. I did not catch him, and when I returned to my bunk, my soup was gone. Another thief had stolen it, so I had to go without any food for the next two days.

Nevertheless, Michael retains a starkly realistic appraisal of the thief's dilemma. "In a way you can't blame these thieves. It was a matter of survival. People with a lot of scruples didn't make it. If you didn't look out for yourself, you didn't survive."

Michael remained in Flossenbürg for about five weeks until a group of prisoners were marched to another camp at Leonberg (near Stuttgart), which was guarded by Hungarian soldiers.[4] He remembers that

the Hungarians knew that their German allies were losing the war. They no longer had any heart in guarding us. Everything was disorganized. I picked my own barrack and slept where I wanted. After about a week I was taken to a nearby underground airplane factory that consisted of a two-level tunnel dug deep into the mountains. The Allies dropped bombs there, but it was well protected. I was assigned to drill and rivet airplane wings. The work was hard, but at least it was inside away from the cold. I remained there for two to three weeks until we were evacuated as the British and French Armies approached from the west. I knew that the war would end with a German defeat and that I only had to hold out another month or two.

After that I was marched to another camp, but I can't recall its name. I had never seen this type of camp before. There were no barracks, only underground windowless rooms dug deep into the ground. They were lighted with electricity. The camp was divided with a wire fence. On the other side was a camp for female prisoners. Like the men, their heads were shaved, and they looked very undernourished. It was good, however, to see that some women were still alive. We talked to them through the fence, which was a novelty, for I had not spoken to a woman since I had arrived at Auschwitz.

I stayed in that camp for about two weeks and was then transported by train to another camp in Bavaria called Mildorf. By then it was already spring and getting warmer. From the Mildorf camp we were taken daily to the Mildorf train depot. It was a very busy station, and we worked on the docks loading and unloading coal. Several times Allied planes came and bombed the train and rails. During one of these raids, when we were fixing the rails, the planes flew especially low and machine-gunned everything and everybody in sight. I dropped to the ground and observed bullets hitting the ground all around me. I don't know how I managed not to get hit. Luckily I wasn't, although others were, including guards and prisoners.

Michael was now more hopeful about being liberated by the Allies, but he also regrets their disregard for the lives of the prisoners:

Although the Allied bombing put our lives in danger, I didn't mind it since the aim was to destroy equipment that was important to the German war effort. However, I really didn't understand the machine-gunning. This I found senseless. Didn't they realize that we were prisoners? It was clear that the Allies didn't come to save our lives, and I could have gotten killed at the last minute for nothing. At the same time I was happy about the prospects of my liberation.

Finally toward the end of April we boarded a train again. The train had a couple of cars loaded with war equipment — artillery, guns, tanks, and other vehicles — attached after every second car of prisoners. We were traveling around for days, our destination unknown to us. I was beginning to feel feverish and sick with what I later learned was typhus.

Suddenly another air raid occurred. The Allies bombed the train indiscriminately, destroying much of the equipment. Unfortunately, they also hit the prisoner cars, and many were killed. Again, however, I did not mind the bombing, for it was another sign that the Germans were being defeated. We looked around and there was not a guard in sight; they had run away. Many of us got off the train and took off into a nearby village. I went with a few others to a home of a German family and asked for food. We were given bread. The occupants looked at us as if we had come from Mars and appeared to be scared of us, expecting us to take revenge. I rested awhile, thinking I was a free man. But my freedom lasted only about an hour, for the guards soon reappeared and, with the help of some old farmers armed with shotguns and pistols, rounded us up and returned us to the train, where they forced us to remove the debris caused by the air raid.

LIBERATION AT LAST

Michael boarded the train again and rode for several more days. As he recalls:

I believe that we were headed for the Tyrol Mountains [among Switzerland, Austria, and Italy], where we were probably going to be killed. Suddenly the train stopped. We couldn't see anything but heard firing in the distance. We didn't move, and after several hours the cars were unlocked. There were a number of German officers with Red Cross emblems. All the SS guards had disappeared. We were told to be patient and that the American Army would be arriving soon.

It was nighttime, so we sat and waited. In the morning the first American troops arrived. They unloaded cans of food and told us to wait for the second wave. Then they took off chasing the retreating Germans. A few hours later a platoon of American soldiers commanded by a captain arrived, bringing with them captured German Red Cross ambulances operated by German soldiers and officers. The captain ordered the Germans from the Red Cross to administer first aid to the prisoners.

It was May of 1945. The place of our liberation was Tutsing, Bavaria. Nearby was a resort named Feldafing. Feldafing fronted a large lake with splendid villas on the shores. There was also a hospital there. The villas were occupied by German officers of higher rank who were recuperating from war injuries. The American captain ordered the Germans to be evacuated out of the villas and hospital. All hospital personnel, including doctors, nurses, and orderlies, were ordered to remain. The captain put them in charge of the sick prisoners with a stern warning: Should any of us die because of their negligence, they would answer to him. He also made it known that he was an American Jew from New York. That announcement made quite an impression on us as well as the Germans. They did not expect any sympathy from him.

I had a feeling of elation to see that a Jew could have such power over the Germans. I had always felt that Jews were better off in the United States. The fact that a Jew could hold such an important position in the American Army only reinforced this belief. In the Polish Army Jews were not considered capable of being good soldiers and were not allowed to rise to a rank higher than sergeant, unless you were a medical doctor. This ate away at our self-esteem and made us feel inferior. Now I had a feeling of pride to know that Jews had contributed to the Allied military effort.

I moved into a villa with several other boys. They were all furnished with comfortable beds. We were finally free men! A large communal kitchen that previously served the Germans was now used for us. The captain stationed American soldiers all around the place to supervise and guard us against any German soldiers who might still try to attack us. Of course, they all disappeared. Some of the healthy prisoners, I believe they were Greek Jews, took off into the woods after some of the Germans, although this was not officially permitted. There were rumors in the camp that they caught several SS guards and killed them.

Michael's liberation by the American troops was quite clearly a desirable status passage. Yet even at this point his survival remained tenuous:

We were not used to the rich food, and many of us got sick. I had already been feeling feverish since the transport. I was taken to the hospital, where I was diagnosed as having typhus. For two weeks I ran a high temperature and was unconscious most of the time. When the fever broke, I found myself in a comfortable bed being taken care of by German female nurses. They told me that they had not expected me to live. But I had, and with good care I was on my way to becoming fully recovered. Five weeks later I was discharged from the hospital and returned to the villa. I was getting stronger, and my hair had grown back. I sat around the lake taking it all in. I received new civilian clothing and kept the striped prison shirt for a souvenir.

One summer morning, on a Sunday, my roommates came for me at the lake to tell me that an American soldier was looking for me. I ran back to the villa and saw a soldier and a corporal sitting in a jeep. The corporal introduced himself as Bernard Fabian from Chicago, whom I immediately knew as my first cousin (the son of my mother's brother, Hersch Leib). He had emigrated to America from Krosno when he was about ten years old and I was about five. He was still able to converse in Polish.

As one can imagine, the transition to a normal life was very difficult for the displaced Jews. Help from family and friends was an important factor in making this transition relatively easier.[5] This is how Bernard had managed to find Michael:

As soon as I was liberated, I gave the Red Cross the name of my sister Frances, who was living in Los Angeles. I did not know her address, only that she lived in L.A. and that her husband's name was William Schneider. Apparently it did not take long to find them and inform them that I was alive and residing in a displaced person camp in Feldafing. Frances immediately wrote to several cousins from New York and Chicago who were serving among the American occupying forces in Germany. My cousin Bernard was the first to receive the information. His first Sunday off, he took a jeep and driver and came to see me. He told me that Frances had written that Shlomo was alive and had contacted them from Italy. Now that was the best of news!

After talking for several hours, Bernard said he had to return to his unit, for he only had a one-day pass. I couldn't let him go just like that, so I asked if I could go with him. He had a conference with his friend. I could not understand any English, so I did not know what they were saying. But finally he said, "Go and get your things. You're coming with me." I responded, "What you see is what I got." So I climbed aboard and off we went. We traveled several hours on the autobahn and arrived at a town in the region of Ulm, where his division was stationed. Bernard had a brief conversation with the guards at the entrance, and we were passed on. We went straight to a bungalow that he occupied with several of his friends. I received the most enthusiastic welcome from them. I could not converse in English, but Bernard interpreted for me. They nicknamed me "Polski."

In the morning Bernard went to see his captain and explain that I was his cousin who had survived the concentration camps. The captain was very sympathetic and told Bernard to take me to the supply house to get me a uniform, for officially he could not allow any civilians to stay with the troops. I was issued a complete uniform, including a helmet — everything but a firearm.

Michael's initial impressions of the Americans were very positive, which contributed to his resolve to come to the United States. He remembers Bernard taking him to the mess hall for breakfast. "I was familiar with what Polish, Russian, and German soldiers ate for breakfast, and compared to the Americans, they ate like paupers. The Americans had eggs, bacon, hotcakes, and coffee. And they could eat all they wanted. Now I definitely knew where I wanted to go — America!"

However, Michael did experience one disappointment that stuck in his mind: "When I first entered the mess hall, I spotted a black American soldier eating by himself in the kitchen, while the rest of the white soldiers were eating in the dining room. I asked my cousin why he was eating alone. Bernard just answered, 'Don't ask any questions.' Later he told me that the black soldier didn't belong to this division but only delivered provisions from the outside. Besides, he explained, the American armed forces were segregated."

Michael stayed with Bernard for about four weeks and began to pick up a little English. When Bernard was ordered to the United States after completing his tour of duty, Michael was allowed to stay until the whole division left a few weeks later. He recalls feeling that "I was now on my own, alone in Germany."

I returned to Feldafing, where I found out that another cousin of mine had been looking for me. He was Captain Bernard Buchwald from New York, the son of my mother's sister Yetta. He did not leave an address but only a message that I could find him in the military government in Augsburg, Bavaria, near Munich. I went to Augsburg only to find that my cousin had returned to New York. He did, however, leave with a friend, who was a lieutenant, an envelope with papers for me. In the envelope I found an affidavit from Frances which indicated that she would guarantee financial support if I was allowed into the U.S., as well as my travel fare to get there. Frances also gave me instructions to take the papers to the American consul in Munich and to register for immigration to the USA.

The American consul informed me that I would be notified in due time when my visa would be issued and transportation would be available. In Munich there was an organization that kept track of survivors living in Germany. I learned that my cousin Fred Seiden, whom I had met in the Oranienburg camp, was living in a little town called Trotsberg. I went to see him and stayed there until July of 1946.

Fred and five other prisoners had come to Trotsberg after escaping from the Death Marches. They were aided there by a young woman named Maria and her family, who hid them out for about a week until the American troops arrived. Fred had lost his wife and child during the war and was quite ill at the time of his liberation. Maria nursed him back to good health. The two of them developed quite an affection for each other, and they eventually married and emigrated to the United States.

During the war Maria had been harassed by people in her town for fraternizing with foreign civilian workers. At one time she was almost arrested by the Nazis for her association with a Frenchman. While I was staying in Trotsberg, both Fred and Maria were beaten up by some local townspeople who resented German girls who associated with foreigners. Fred was beaten so badly that he almost died. He was in the hospital for almost two weeks but eventually recovered.

For the most part, however, Michael found the German population friendly during his stay in Germany:

They all claimed that they didn't know anything about the extermination camps. Everyone was completely innocent; no one admitted to being a Nazi. In reality I think they were scared that we would take revenge against them. But they were very nice and helpful. Some Jews even boarded with German families.

I made friends with both Jews and Germans. I ate in restaurants and sat around in beer halls. Food was being rationed to everyone at the time, but survivors were issued double the coupons that were being given to Germans. Thus, we actually had more food than the rest of the population. There was also a thriving black market in Germany, and there was a lot of jewelry that was circulating. It was a natural thing for some of us to start trading. I learned how to get American cigarettes, coffee, and chocolate bars. We tried to live it up as much as possible.

My friends and I were especially fond of the German girls. Because of our black market activities, we had a lot to offer them that they didn't have. Whether or not it was genuine, they seemed to like us. So when I traveled around to different cities, I usually had a girlfriend who invited me into her home to stay with her family. At this point I began to lose my feelings of rage toward all Germans for what had happened to me. I knew that if I had come across certain people, I would have killed them. But I didn't generalize this to those who weren't responsible. I also had little interest in going back to Poland at the time. I knew that no one from my family had survived there, and I had heard about a group of survivors who had been attacked and murdered by some Poles at Kielce.[6]

One of the incidents Michael remembers best during this transitional period of his life involved a young German woman named Heidi:

I met Heidi while she was traveling with a friend in Trotsberg. One time I visited her in her hometown near Düsseldorf. We went to a dance where a live orchestra was playing. While we were dancing, somebody turned off the lights in the dance hall, and a bunch of German boys (in their twenties) grabbed Heidi away from me. I started fighting back and was pushed up against a wall. I kept blindly hitting back and finally managed to get onto the podium with the orchestra and started screaming that they were going to be held responsible for this. Then the lights were turned back on, and the orchestra players pulled the guys away from me. I saw that the German boys were holding Heidi and cutting off her hair with scissors. This practice was also done in France and Poland with women who had fraternized with Germans during the war. It was like being a traitor. In Germany it was the same thing. They objected when foreigners associated with their German girls.

I was angry! I knew that nearby was a garrison of Polish troops who were part of the occupying Allied powers. I went there and told them what had happened. It made them angry, too, and they asked me when the next dance was going to be held. The following Sunday I went to the dance. The Polish soldiers arrived, disrupted the whole affair, and beat up a lot of Germans. It was my revenge.

Michael received his U.S. visa in July 1946 and was told by the American consul to report to Bremerhaven for emigration:

> The ship that I sailed on was a converted U.S. troopship. I arrived in New York in September. I was met at the ship by my cousin Bernard Buchwald, who took me home to meet my Aunt Yetta. In New York I also met my father's sister Hinda, and her husband, Chaim Hocheiser. They had lived in New York for many years, and I knew of them. They had a son, an American lieutenant in the air force, who was killed in the war. Chaim said he had lost a son but had gained a nephew whom he would have expected to be dead.
>
> My sister Eleanor came with her husband, Jack Weissbluth, and their five-year-old daughter, Sandy, from Los Angeles to take me by car back with them. After two weeks in New York we stopped for a week in Chicago, where I met many members of my family, including my cousin Bernard Fabian. I arrived in Los Angeles in October and have been living there ever since.

AN UNCERTAIN DESTINY

Like Michael, Shlomo eventually settled in Los Angeles. But he had not originally intended this destination, for he had hoped to go to Palestine. His inability to accomplish this illustrates a case in which, in spite of all his efforts, personal agency could not surmount the constraints of external conditions. In this concluding portion of his narrative, Shlomo describes his experiences from the time he left the Soviet Army in March 1945 to search for survivors in Krosno to the time of his arrival in Los Angeles:

> When I returned to Krosno, I found about twenty-five to thirty Jews living there who had survived by hiding one way or another. Some of them were not actually from our town but from neighboring areas. I went to see the Duchowskis to thank them for helping me. When I knocked at the door, Mr. Duchowski looked at me and said, "Is that you? How come you're wearing a Russian uniform? Did you have to

become a Red?" I knew that Mr. Duchowski did not like the communists, but I replied, "I needed it to survive. And I still need it to survive." It was a pleasant reunion, and they let me sleep there for two
days because I was still apprehensive about revealing myself as a Jew to
others.

Later I went to see the Pole who had taken over our tailor shop and
home. Our house was no longer there; it had been leveled. But this
Pole had inherited everything else we had. All I wanted, however, were
some pictures that I had left behind, which I was able to obtain.

While Shlomo was in Krosno, he learned of a group called Bricha
that was operating in Krosno. Bricha, also known as Beriha, means
"flight" or "escape" in Hebrew.[7] The Beriha movement involved
about 250,000 Jewish survivors, over 48,000 from Poland alone,
who attempted to emigrate illegally to Palestine. The Soviet Union,
which was tightening its control over eastern Europe, officially pro-
hibited the emigration but halfheartedly allowed it. According to
Shlomo:

> Two Bricha leaders from Vilna were stationed in Krosno. Being close to
> the border of southern Poland, Krosno was one of the last places that
> refugees passing into Czechoslovakia, Romania, and Hungary stopped.
> Groups of ten to fifteen Jews, mostly survivors of the concentration
> camps, were being funneled through Krosno and given false identifica-
> tion papers.
>
> I met with the Bricha leaders, and they asked me to assist them.
> With my Russian uniform I could get around relatively easy. For about
> a month I traveled through Poland to Warsaw, Lublin, and Kraków,
> leading small groups of concentration camp survivors to Krosno,
> where they were helped to cross the border into other countries and,
> hopefully, eventually to Palestine.
>
> It was in Kraków, at the headquarters of the Jewish Committee that I
> met my wife, whose name was Gusta Friedman. Gusta had gone to the
> committee to try to get information about her family. She was from
> Tarnopol in eastern Poland. Gusta was blond with blue eyes and had
> survived the war passing as a Pole by the name of Stanisława Urbańska.
> She had been incarcerated for about a year in a prison for Polish politi-
> cal prisoners and had worked as a maid for a German family.
>
> When I first saw Gusta, I fell in love right away. I said to myself, I'm
> going to marry this girl. It was there that I made up my mind to leave

the Soviet Army and travel with Gusta to Palestine. When I first asked her out at the Jewish Committee, she refused. I learned that she was staying with the wife of a Polish officer who was stationed in England. They didn't know Gusta was Jewish. I went to the house and knocked on the door. The officer's wife opened the door, and I asked for Stanisława. She said that Stanisława was not home. Apparently she and her husband didn't like the communists, and I was still in a Soviet uniform. I didn't believe her and stuck my foot in the door, looked in, and saw Gusta standing in the room. I pushed myself in, and I asked the woman to leave the room. I told Gusta that I knew she wanted to leave Poland and that she didn't have any money and didn't know anybody who had survived.[8] I told her that I had made up my mind to emigrate and that I wanted her to go with me. I was leaving with a group of people the next morning at 10:00 A.M. to go to Krosno, and from there we were going across the border. If she wanted to go, she should meet me at the Jewish Committee. That was the whole conversation. The next morning, to my great delight, Gusta was there!

At about 12:00 P.M. I took a group to the railroad station at Kraków. A lot of them were still wearing their striped concentration camp uniforms. The train consisted mostly of cattle cars, and all of the passenger cars were filled. However, with the help of a few Soviet soldiers, we opened the door to one of the cars and said, "Everybody out!" After emptying the car of all of the Poles, we boarded and went on to Krosno.

Back in Krosno we were given false documents as surviving Greek Jews. With Gusta I took a group of survivors in an open-car freight train out of Poland. Before crossing the border into Czechoslovakia, I took off my army uniform, threw it off the train, and tore up all of my army documents. I put on civilian clothing that I had had made for me in Krosno and became Shlomo Harari, which means "Berger" in Hebrew, a Greek concentration camp survivor.

Our first destination was the Hungarian town of Debrecen, where we were to get orders from Bricha regarding our next destination. We arrived in early May and were there for a few days. On May 9 we woke up to a big celebration — cannons firing and music playing. We went out into the streets and found out that Germany had capitulated and that the war in Europe was over!

Two days later we left Debrecen for Romania, where we stopped for a few days in the town of Klusz on the Romania-Hungary border. All through our trip I had been asking Gusta to marry me. She finally agreed, and we were married on May 18 by a Jewish rabbi.

Our next stop was Bucharest, where we planned to board a ship at Constanţa on the Black Sea. When we arrived, however, we were told by Bricha that the ships were now in Italy. They gave us forged International Red Cross passports for stateless people. I kept my name Harari, but I was now listed as Italian.

From there we were sent to Belgrade in Yugoslavia. We expected to be put on a plane and fly across the Adriatic Sea to Bari in southern Italy. However, the Yugoslavs had stopped the flights, for what reasons I am unsure. We stayed at the Jewish Center in Belgrade for about two to three weeks. Then a group of us were issued train tickets to travel to Italy. We traveled through Yugoslavia and Croatia into Trieste and up to the northern part of Italy until we arrived at Bologna.

In Bologna there was a transit camp that had been taken over by the Jewish Brigade of Palestine. They took charge of us and gave everyone new documents. They put us on a train and sent us south for about a three-day ride. We settled in southern Italy in a displaced persons camp right on the sea in Santa Maria di Bagni. While we waited to get into Palestine, we organized protest demonstrations every day in front of the British Consulate to urge them to grant us independence.

By August 1945 there were about fifteen thousand Jews in displaced persons camps in Italy.[9] Shlomo and Gusta were among the first to arrive in Santa Maria di Bagni. According to Shlomo, "There were only a couple hundred people when we arrived. We established a kibbutz and lived in one large building with a communal kitchen. Some people went out to work and contributed whatever money they made to the collective. At various times during the middle of the night twenty or thirty of us were selected, put into little boats, and taken to small ships that were waiting offshore."

Shlomo was not privy to how the Jewish leadership made decisions about who would be selected to go to Palestine. But people were sometimes turned down because they lacked a strong commitment to Zionism.[10] Shlomo believes that politics was a factor in his case as well. As he says, "For political reasons Gusta and I were always left out. One of the first things the Jewish Brigade had us do was to register and indicate our former Zionist affiliations. I registered my affiliation as Betar, and it appeared that the left-wing Zionists were given priority." Thus, Shlomo's prewar affiliation with the right-wing of the Zionist movement was a disadvantage, rather than a resource, that prevented him from obtaining his intended objective of entering Palestine.

Shlomo recalls waiting in Santa Maria di Bagni for about three years. In the meantime Gusta got pregnant. He says that "if we had been selected before then, we probably would have ended up in Palestine." But now "I feared putting Gusta through the risks of an illegal immigration." Jack, their son, was born on August 24, 1946.[11] In retrospect, Shlomo is glad he didn't go to Palestine "because I think our lives would have been much harder there."

Like Michael, Shlomo also received help from his family in the United States. When Gusta got pregnant, he got in touch with his sister Frances in Los Angeles:

> I remembered the address of her cleaning store and gave an American soldier I met in Italy a letter for her, which he sent through the military mail. I had also sent her a letter through the Red Cross. Frances received the letters and wrote back, informing me that Michael had survived and was living in Germany. She also sent us affidavits of support and plane tickets to come to America.
>
> The American Consulate opened up for registration in Naples in October of 1946. When we found out that there was going to be a registration for emigration, I immediately took the train to Naples. I waited all night in front of the American Consulate. At about 9:00 A.M. they opened the door and started the registration. By that time I had returned to using my original name. I got the three of us registered on the Polish list, and we were given numbers 182, 183, and 184. I thought these were good numbers because the Polish list had about 6,500 persons. Unfortunately, they closed the Polish visas at about 50.

Thus, for awhile Shlomo and his family lived in limbo between the past and the future. The eventual resolution of this predicament was not entirely of Shlomo's own doing but was dependent on the actions of others:

> I took a job with ORT [Organization for Rehabilitation Through Training] as a clothing design instructor for two years. Through my ORT job I met a Jewish girl from England who was a welfare officer for UNRA [United Nations Relief Agency]. She told me she could get us to England if we wanted to leave. Since we had no way of getting into

America at that time — and with a baby I didn't want to go illegally into Palestine — I agreed. She sent a letter to her brother-in-law in England, and within two weeks we received a request to come to England as a domestic-resident couple. I went to the Polish Consulate, where we were issued three new passports as Polish citizens, and then to the English Consulate, where we were given a temporary six-month visa.

The UNRA worker's brother-in-law had no intention of hiring us as domestic servants. But Gusta had found out through the Red Cross that she had an aunt who had survived and was living in London. When we arrived in London, the brother-in-law picked us up at the train depot and took us to Gusta's aunt. We lived with her while we were there, and the brother-in-law got me a job at the tailor shop where he ordered his clothes. The owner of the tailor shop went with me to the labor department and signed us up as a domestic couple.

After six months in England we were supposed to get an extension of our visas. At that time a police officer came to our house and told Gusta that he would like me to come to the police station and to bring all my documents. I wasn't home, but the next Saturday I went down to the station. The officer looked at the papers and said, "You're supposed to be a domestic resident couple. How come you live here?" I said, "Well, these people have a small house. They don't mind if we live outside as long as I go to work every day." He asked me another few questions, took all the documents, and said to wait five minutes. He came back and gave us a permanent residency.

Within five years we could have become citizens of England. But all of a sudden in 1950 we received a letter from the American Consulate that our registration number from Italy was under consideration for emigration. We went to the consulate, got our visas, and liquidated everything we had. We bought tickets on a luxury liner called the *New Amsterdam* and came to New York in May of 1950. From New York we took the train all the way to Los Angeles, where we have lived up to this day.

CHAPTER 7

Conclusion

Elie Wiesel has expressed concern that the discourse of social science will inevitably fail to communicate the nature of the evil and suffering that were the Holocaust.[1] In some of his own work Wiesel has struggled with his personal disappointment with God and his simultaneous reverence toward God.[2] Even though his writings have now "achieved a reverential, even sacramental status for Holocaust literature,"[3] he writes about the Holocaust "to denounce writing."[4]

Most historians respect Wiesel's position and acknowledge that the "horrors and brutalities" of the Holocaust are difficult to comprehend "because we cannot imagine ourselves experiencing them."[5] Yet historians caution against seeing the Holocaust as an inexplicable event that occurred "outside" history. In recent years they have come a long way toward demystifying the Holocaust and bringing it into the mainstream of their discipline. Wiesel's admonition notwithstanding, sociologists need to do the same.

A THEORETICAL SUMMARY

Gerald Markle and associates argue that attempts at sociological generalization about survivors' experiences "deny the singular humanity of each survivor." They believe that each account "stands alone as a document of the Holocaust," that each "paints its own picture, delivers its unique tale." According to Markle et al., social scientists are trained to find patterns within chaos, to "conflate experience into category." Yet Markle et al. remain "convinced that there is no common theory . . . [or] grand narrative . . . which capture[s] survivors' particular experiences. . . . [T]here is no universal story, no . . . universal experience of 'the Holocaust survivor,' . . . no list of variables which, once identified, would light that awful darkness."[6]

Respectfully, however, I argue that this observation tends toward mystification, for the same could be said of all biographical experience. The particularity of individual experience is not, in my view, necessarily at odds with general sociological explanation. The problem with much sociological theorizing is that it is not grounded in individual experience. This is what makes the life history method in sociology so important and what makes it necessary to begin a sociological analysis of Jewish Holocaust survival at the most general level of explanation — at the level of fundamental presuppositional categories that do not presume analytic closure over a phenomenon that "remains indeterminate, elusive, and opaque."[7]

Thus, in this study I have argued that the life history of two brothers' survival affords opportunities to examine one of the central problems of general social theory: the relationship between human agency and social structure. As a sensitizing scheme that allows incorporation of interactionist concepts, these presuppositional categories provide a foundation for developing a distinctly sociological alternative to the psychological theorizing that has dominated the survivor literature and to characterizations of Jews that are overly negative or overly heroic.

The agency-structure framework emerged in the course of the research. I adopted a "narrative interview" approach to collecting the life histories by first asking the Berger brothers to reconstruct their experiences and then prompting them to expand their narratives to fill in gaps. Michael and Shlomo's accounts were still accessible because of the numerous, varied, and enduring emotional reminders of the Holocaust epiphanies they had experienced, including crucial moments in which their ability to make difficult choices and quick decisions was the difference between life and death. These situations illuminated the relationship between agency and structure in instances in which the tension between them was heightened.

The Berger brothers and other Jews who survived the Holocaust did so in the face of a social structure that was systematically organized by the Nazi regime to accomplish their deaths. Michael and Shlomo's ability to exercise agency successfully was influenced by their prewar exposure to cultural schemas and resources that they were able to transpose to the war-occupation context. Knowledge of non-Jewish cultural schemas such as language and religion was especially important to Shlomo's survival outside of the camps, where he operated in a closed awareness context and needed to maintain a front as a Christian Pole. In the camps Michael operated in an open awareness context, where he needed to impress his captors that he was someone who could perform productive labor for them.

Perhaps the most important resources the brothers had at their disposal were the tailoring skills they had acquired as youths, which they were able to exchange for favors and provisions both inside and outside the camps. Michael and Shlomo were also socialized in a family cultural milieu where flexibility and willingness to take risks, as indicated by their siblings who had emigrated, were normative. As children they were not isolated from the Christian population and had acquired knowledge of non-Jewish cultural schemas that was a resource for negotiating situations with non-Jews. In part because of their religious agnosticism and experience with Zionist youth movements, they were not fatalistic about God's role in helping them survive. Both were able to realistically appraise their situation and take strategic courses of action through calculated risk-taking and disobedience. This was not an attitudinal or behavioral trait that came easily to many Jews, for after centuries of persecution "Jews had learned that in order to survive they had to refrain from resistance."[8] In addition, Michael and Shlomo's age was itself a resource that maximized their capacity to endure physical hardship and withstand disease. Moreover, the step-by-step process of their disempowerment allowed the brothers time to acquire experience living under German occupation that could later be used as a resource to help them survive.

However, the Berger brothers' ability to exercise their structurally formed capacity for agency successfully was also an interpersonal accomplishment. Both Michael and Shlomo eventually underwent desirable status passages by becoming members of collectivities (such as the Polish Partisans, the Soviet Army, and Kommando 1) that

afforded them increased power and protection from their antagonists. In addition, they benefited from many individual acts of assistance, great and small. At various points during the war Michael and
Shlomo received help from family members, acquaintances, and
strangers. Some acts of aid provided the brothers with essential material resources, and some consisted simply of words of encouragement or expressions of moral support that helped the brothers retain
their sense of self, avoid psychological disintegration, preserve their
faith in humanity, and maintain hope to continue their struggle to
survive.

In the early war years, for example, there were Jewish families
who took Michael and Shlomo into their homes when the brothers
were traveling outside of Krosno. There were times when relatives
(including their mother) who had contacts with the authorities
helped them avoid arrest and imprisonment. The importance of their
father's memorable parting words as he was taken to his death —
"Children, save yourselves!" — cannot be underestimated. Later
when Shlomo was traveling to meet Mr. Duchowski, he met a
stranger whose remark — "If I didn't recognize you as a Jew, nobody
else will" — helped give him confidence that he could pass as a Pole.
Of course, Mr. and Mrs. Duchowski must be credited as central fig-
ures in Shlomo's survival.

In the camps Michael's friendship with Herman was a source of
both material and emotional support. Important as well to Michael's
survival at Buna were the orderly who advised him to request his
release from the hospital, the doctor who gave him a reprieve from a
crucial selection, the record keeper who gave him a transfer to Kommando 1, and the *Kapo* who helped him become an organizer. During
the Death March Michael's brief encounter with his cousin Fred
Seiden was also a source of inspiration to go on in spite of obstacles.

Even after liberation the brothers' reintegration into postwar
society was aided by the actions of others. Michael, for instance, was
helped by his cousin Bernard Fabian, who took him out of the displaced persons camp. Similarly, Fred Seiden provided Michael with a
familial relationship at a time when he had no other contacts in Germany. As for Shlomo, his relationship with Gusta stands out as the
most significant emotional bond of the postwar period. Importantly,
both brothers' ultimate fate was intimately tied to their sister

Frances's efforts to bring them to the United States. Finally Michael and Shlomo's relationship with each other should be mentioned for the mutual support they lent each other in the early war years. In addition, knowledge along the way that the other was still alive was an invaluable consolation after the loss of their parents.

But in spite of their (and others') best efforts, the Berger brothers were not always able to accomplish their intended objectives. The emergent realm of social reality into which they were propelled was marked by epiphanic moments whose outcome they could not anticipate. They experienced numerous occasions where the opportunity to exercise agency eluded them and they could have easily been killed. They believe that their survival was very much contingent on factors that were beyond their control, which they view, as do other survivors, as a matter of luck or miracles. Nevertheless, the agency that was constituted by their and other survivors' ability to hold on, to hope that good luck would come their way, was itself a resource that may have derived from accumulated experience. As Viktor Frankl observes, "Even if we could not expect any sensational military events in the next few days, *who knew better than we, with our experience of camps,* how great chances sometimes opened up, quite suddenly, at least for the individual. . . . For this was the kind of thing which constituted the 'luck' of the prisoner."[9] Thus, what survivors understand as luck does not, in my view, deny the significance of agency in overcoming structural conditions of extremity or other forms of adversity.

At the same time the Berger brothers' life history suggests it would be unwise to overestimate individuals' ability to overcome structural conditions of extremity and assign privileged status to agency over structure in social analyses. If Germany had not been defeated in the war, Michael, Shlomo, and the other Jewish survivors would have inevitably perished. Their liberation was essentially a by-product of the Allies' defeat of the Nazis.[10] Moreover, Jewish survival of the Holocaust remains a "fragmentary achievement," for even in its most "triumphant guise" the agency exercised by survivors contrasts sharply with their impotence in the face of family loss.[11] Hitler and the Nazis essentially accomplished their goal of removing Jews from many parts of Europe in which Jewish life and culture had flourished. In Poland in particular, as Sophie Caplan observes, "there remains only a vestigial Jewish community in Warsaw, Cracow, and Lublin, mostly over age seventy, with small groups of younger people, most of them intermarried, and a larger group of 'underground' Jews who do not wish to reveal their true identity. Unless there is drastic change, in twenty years' time Jewish life in Poland will have ended."[12]

MEMORIES OF SUFFERING, THE POLITICS OF VICTIMIZATION, AND POSTMODERN SENSIBILITY

Geoffrey Hartman suggests that life is marked by "a contradictory effort: to remember and to forget, to respect the past and to acknowledge that the present is open to the future."[13] Anne Roiphe adds, "We want to forget [the Holocaust], to ignore, to go on, and yet we remain preoccupied."[14] Michael and Shlomo cannot forget the horror and suffering they endured, but they have refused to live the rest of their lives dwelling on the past. At times the notion of "survivor guilt" so prevalent in the literature even seems a piteous indulgence.[15] Put simply, in Michael's words, "I never felt guilty about being alive. That's poor reasoning. It wouldn't do the dead any good, and it's not what my parents would have wanted. My father always said, 'Save yourself. Don't worry about me!'" Shlomo remarks, "We came here and made a new life. And life has been good to us. We could have never accomplished in Poland or any other place what we did in America. We established ourselves economically. We educated our children. We did the best that we could."

Psychiatrist Shamai Davidson has examined a number of factors that have influenced survivors' adjustment to postwar society:

> For many survivors who had been married and had children before the Holocaust, the multiple losses . . . created colossal burdens of mourning. . . . A further particularly vulnerable group . . . were young children. . . . The deprivation resulting from separation and loss of parental figures in early childhood often had a serious effect on psychological development. . . . However, a majority of survivors did not become psychiatric patients and have shown remarkable capacities in overcoming the effect of the extreme experiences and multiple

losses, creating new lives and healthy and successful, well-integrated families.[16]

Davidson's research indicates that those who were in their teens or twenties, like the Berger brothers, seem "to have . . . made the best recovery. . . . Survivor syndrome symptoms were present only to a minor extent and survivor guilt was not as pronounced. The loss of their families came at a time when separation from parents [under normal conditions] is a stage in the life cycle in the development towards autonomy."[17]

Thus, like so many of the other 140,000 Jewish survivors who came to the United States after they were liberated, Michael and Shlomo established successful work and family lives.[18] Although these lives have not been without problems, it is difficult to attribute these to the Holocaust per se rather than to those problems that might be encountered by any other group of immigrants or people with a legacy of suffering. Survivors' accounts can help inform us about the ways in which individuals who have endured hardship overcome adversity. Sociologists have spent a good deal of time debunking ideologies that blame the disadvantaged and oppressed for their own victimization but have neglected to examine this fundamental dimension of human behavior.[19]

Joseph Amato notes that stories of personal suffering are universal and, as collective memories, are "commingled with the stories of mass society, nations, and their institutions."[20] However, in the United States and elsewhere around the world various groups compete with each other to exchange their moral status as victims for public deference and compensatory resources.[21] In the post-Holocaust world victimization has become a political commodity and the Holocaust survivor a metaphor for all victims of prejudice, discrimination, and injustice. Every group stakes out a claim for its own "holocaust." Some feminists, for instance, describe women's experience in society as universally victimizing and women's subordination as comparable to Jews' experience under Nazism.[22] The metaphor of the Holocaust survivor is even used to describe the situation of adult children of alcoholics.[23] Increasingly this competition of victimhood has become divisive and rather disconcerting. For example, Na'im Akbar, an African-American scholar, contends that it is a "simplistic notion of slavery which makes it easy for people to compare their holocaust to our holocaust. They don't understand that going to the ovens knowing who you are, is damn well better than walking around for 100 years not knowing who you are. . . . Our holocaust in America is worse than the holocaust in Europe."[24]

Moreover, this politics of victimization confronts the American ethic of individualism and self-reliance and often fails, promoting public backlash precisely because it seems to deny individuals' capacity to exercise agency to overcome adversity. At times it also trivializes the "difference between holocausts that happen only metaphorically and holocausts that happen in fact."[25]

Some Jews have also appropriated the memory of the Holocaust for political purposes and have "developed a vested interest in establishing the Holocaust as 'unique.'"[26] In what Michael Marrus and Jacob Neusner refer to as "the triumphalism of pain" or "the salvific myth," some Jews argue that "the Holocaust must be understood as a period of torment and disaster prior to redemption — realized in the achievement of the State of Israel."[27] To be sure, as Roiphe observes, "The State of Israel owes the timing of its political reality . . . to the Holocaust. . . . The Western countries in a moment of guilty conscience allowed Israel to exist, to end the Jewish problem, to pay homage to the dead who would not have died had there been an Israeli consulate to stamp visas and an Israeli prime minister who could pick up the phone and speak to heads of states."[28] However, Roiphe and others express concern that the Holocaust has become a "banal instrument" for the legitimation of particular Israeli policies.[29] It is invoked to promote political cohesion within Israel and to appeal to American Jews for unconditional support. Some Jews liken the Palestinians to Nazis and equate compromise with them "to Munich and the abandonment of Czechoslovakia in 1938."[30]

Recent reports indicate that the younger generations of Israeli Jews are less likely than their elders to find the Holocaust as central to their identity or as sufficient a basis on which to formulate foreign policy vis-à-vis their adversaries.[31] Some Jews may find this trend disconcerting, but much more troublesome is the way in which the memory of the Holocaust has been turned back against Israel and appropriated for anti-Jewish objectives. In an obvious effort to delegitimize the Jewish state, anti-Israel media campaigns make free use of Nazi metaphors and equate Zionism to Nazism. For example, Luai Abdo, a Palestine Liberation Organization magazine editor, has published articles claiming that the Holocaust is Zionist propaganda and that "Nazi camps were more 'civilized' than Israeli prisons."[32] Such propagandists understand quite well how to manipulate the memory of the Holocaust. As Roiphe writes:

> The cry of "Zionism is racism" is an attempt by the Arab countries and their sympathizers to undo the moral right of the Jews to their land, to take away from Jews the justification of history for their new nation. If Zionists are no better than Nazis, . . . both unjustly oppressing a minority who live within its borders, then the basis of granting the new state its legality is eroded away and all the world can join together in taking back this gift of guilt . . . because the Jews have demonstrated that they are not victims but brutes. . . . [It is as if] the entitlement that the Jews had won through their suffering in the Holocaust . . . has now been finished and the world is relieved. Jews no longer victims, no longer have a moral club to wield over anyone else. Now they are wielding real clubs like everyone else.[33]

Perhaps Jews can take some solace in surveys that indicate that the public in the United States "generally views the Holocaust with concern and understanding."[34] In a 1990 poll conducted by Yankelovich Clancy Shulman, of which 97.5 percent of the respondents were non-Jews, 64 percent agreed that the Holocaust remains relevant for dealing with contemporary moral issues, 73 percent believed that it is important to teach about the Holocaust in schools, and 91 percent felt that everyone should be concerned about what happened to the Jews during the Nazi period.

But Dennis Klein, director of the Anti-Defamation League Center for Holocaust Studies, warns that "we now live with a surfeit of awareness of the Nazi past . . . that . . . can just as easily inundate as illuminate."[35] National surveys conducted by reputable polling organizations in the United States in the mid-1980s found that at least 40 percent of the respondents thought that "Jews should stop focusing on the Holocaust . . . [and] complaining about what happened to them in Nazi Germany."[36] About 33 percent expressed resentment of "the periodic references to the Holocaust in public life, and tend[ed] to attribute these to unwarranted Jewish pressure or influence." Even though the anti-Jewish sentiments expressed in the 1990 Yankelovich survey were somewhat lower — 19 percent indicated that Americans have heard "too much" about the Holocaust, and 26 percent thought it is "relatively unimportant to incorporate the Holocaust into American education" — the evidence suggests that a significant segment of the population remains susceptible to the claims of those who insist on "whitewashing Hitler's regime and denying or trivializing the crimes committed in its name."[37] Thus, a poll conducted by the Roper Organization in the spring of 1993 found that 22 percent believed it was "possible" that "the Nazi extermination of the Jews never happened" and 12 percent said they did not know.[38]

In Germany, moreover, the public demonstrates even more ambivalence toward the Holocaust than in the United States. A 1992 Der Spiegel poll indicated that 62 percent of German respondents hoped for an end to the focus on the Nazi past, 44 percent felt that Hitler had had both good and bad qualities, and 32 percent believed that "Jews were at least partly responsible for the persecution they experienced."[39] There is also a movement within mainstream politics and academe in Germany that attempts to relativize or normalize the Holocaust by equating the experiences of Jews under Nazism to the experiences of persecuted minorities in other countries.[40] Some German historians have constructed a narrative drama in which Germany itself is portrayed as a victim of the war. The Soviet Union is considered responsible for initiating wartime atrocities, and the Allies are blamed for indiscriminately bombing German civilians in genocidal proportions. Ernst Nolte, a philosopher-historian of some notoriety, even suggests that Hitler's actions against the Jews in the German-occupied territories, albeit misguided and exaggerated, were taken in response to Jewish support of the Allied war effort and the threat of Jewish partisan activity behind German lines.[41] It is almost as if the Jewish victims are now turned into perpetrators who are responsible for their own demise. Many Germans believe that their country has been unfairly tarnished and branded as a pariah nation by accusations that they have "collective guilt." (Of course, Jews are blamed for promoting such anti-German sentiments.) Instead Germans want to emphasize their country's positive accomplishments in the postwar years and construct a national identity that can be a source of pride for the German people. President Ronald Reagan made his own contribution to these developments when he visited the German military cemetery at Bitburg in 1985 and "gave the impression of wishing to recall nothing [about World War II] except common sacrifices and a shared code of military honor."[42]

These trends taken as a whole suggest that collective memories of the Holocaust are variable, in flux, and vulnerable to trivialization and misrepresentation. And, of course, there are those who deny that the genocide occurred altogether.[43] They reinforce Jewish fears, as expressed by Elie Wiesel's nightmare — "I wake up shivering, thinking that when we die, no one will be able to persuade people that the Holocaust occurred."[44] They lead George Steiner to feel that "when I listen to my children breathing in the stillness of my house I grow afraid. I am utterly trying to teach the sense of vulnerability and keep them in training for survival."[45]

Omer Bartov, writing in the journal History and Memory, expresses concern about how intellectuals themselves may contribute to this state of affairs and wonders about how "postmodern" social thought will come to grips with the varying collective memories of the Holocaust.[46] Postmodernism is an intellectual movement that challenges and attempts to deconstruct hegemonic structures and ideologies.[47] Postmodern thinkers tend to dispute the possibility of accurately representing social reality in an objective or impartial manner. All knowledge is understood as a social construction underlaid by political interests that seek to legitimate a particular view of the world. The distinction between fact and fiction is dissolved. "Doubt is the essential postmodern sensibility. . . . No discourse is privileged, cynicism reigns."[48] Thus, postmodern thought questions our ability to create a coherent interpretation of the past and derive any moral meaning for the future.

However, Bartov asks, are there not events of the past that exist independently of our own reconstructions? If all versions of the Holocaust are social constructions, are they all equally valid (or invalid)? According to Bartov, proponents of postmodern sensibility "often claim to be fighting a war of liberation against the tyranny of a totalizing discourse. . . . [But their] efforts to come to terms with the amorphous nature of reality can play so easily into the hands of

those who have no qualms about producing realities of the most hor-
rific nature and then claiming that they had never taken place."[49] As
Heinrich Himmler asserted in his infamous speech to his SS troops,
"Most of you . . . know what it means to have seen 100 corpses
together, or 500, or 1,000. To have made one's way through that,
and — some instances of weakness aside — to have remained a
decent person throughout, that is what has made us hard . . .
[and] is a page of our history that will *never be written*."[50] Similarly,
Simon Wiesenthal reports how SS officers in the camps mocked
inmates by saying that "even if some proof should remain and some
of you survive, people will say that the events you describe are too
monstrous to be believed."[51]

Bartov wants intellectuals to consider whether postmodern sensibility itself now makes Holocaust denial more plausible: "Perhaps
what we believed to be interesting, intellectually stimulating, even
playful, when applied to an extreme case proves to be morally dubi-
ous. . . . [If] a murder has taken place, we did not construct it in
our imagination."[52] Does not our desire to ensure that the Holocaust
never again happens assume that the Holocaust did exist as fact and
"could indeed exist as fact again"?[53] Are there no limits whatsoever
to the kinds of stories that can responsibly be told about the Holocaust?[54] Bartov seeks an interpretive framework that gives the analyst
choices other than "a blind and uncritical belief in facts and a wholly
skeptical view" regarding our ability to establish the facticity of the
Holocaust.[55] As John Johnson and David Altheide observe, "To assert
that active human consciousness [and] interpretation . . . have
helped construct an . . . account of some topic, only shows it to be
a human construction; it does not show that it is false or incom-
plete."[56]

What makes the Holocaust appear incomprehensible also makes
its memory elusive. Survivors' accounts are the most effective means
of guarding against forgetting the past. As Hartman notes, "Every
time we retrieve an oral history . . . we are creating a line of resistance against [the] effacement of . . . memory."[57] Collective memories may be social constructions, but there are limits to the kinds of
memories that can be convincingly propagated and afforded legiti-
macy by different publics.[58] Because survivors have been willing to
relive their suffering and tell their stories, their accounts will forever

be available for future generations.[59] In addition to providing the world with emotional reminders of the evil that human beings are capable of inflicting on one another, survivors' stories are "testimonies to the ability of the human being to endure, to prevail, and to triumph over the structural forces that threaten . . . all of us."[60] Elie Wiesel's greatest nightmare need not come true. As one survivor implores us to remember, "Each of us has a different story. All of them true. Believe them."[61]

Epilogue

In the spring of 1989 my father returned to Poland for the first time since the war. My mother, brother, two cousins, and I went with him. My father prepared for our visit for over a year. He began to refamiliarize himself with the Polish language by reading Polish newspapers. He started speaking Polish with a group of Poles he met at the Polish Airlines ticket office in Los Angeles. And he and I began recording his life history.

During our time in Poland we traveled to several cities and towns. We visited my father's hometown in Krosno, the mass grave site where my grandfather is buried, several abandoned Jewish cemeteries, Auschwitz, and other Holocaust memorial sites. It was a moving experience that evoked sadness in all of us. But we were not morose, for the trip was also exhilarating for my father. I could see that he was actually having the time of his life. He talked fondly about his home, school, and places of recreation he had enjoyed as a youth. He loved to talk to people and struck up conversations (in Polish) with strangers wherever we went. One evening during our trip my father told me that he felt that his Auschwitz experience seemed less for naught now that I was writing about it. I was pleased that he thought that the life history project we had undertaken was important and beneficial to him.

When we returned to Los Angeles, we were visited by Eddie Siegal, a family friend who was also a Jewish survivor from Poland. Siegal told us, with some regret in his voice, that his son was not interested in talking about his father's [Eddie's] experience of the Holocaust.[1] He admitted, however, that he'd rather not talk about it himself — "The pain never goes away. . . . I'd rather play cards and try to forget about it." My father replied, "It is good to talk about it, not to deny it, so that you don't feel it was a wasted experience."

Unlike my father, my uncle has never returned to Poland and does not intend to do so. As I said earlier, it appears that the brothers' different modes of survival have left their mark on how they view their native land. My uncle's survival outside of the camps exposed him even more than my father to the actions of anti-Semitic Poles. Nevertheless, like my father, my uncle appreciates the value of undertaking the life history project and of making his story available to his children and grandchildren.

My father did not return to Poland until forty years after the Holocaust. I did not become interested in the Holocaust until I approached forty years of age, a time that in contemporary society represents a transition to mid-life. I find Shamai Davidson's thoughts about the significance of this time dimension provocative: "There are many instances in the Bible where the histories of societies are recorded in . . . forty-year intervals. It seems that in the ancient world a forty-year time lapse was understood to be required by . . . a people in order to reach a perspective on past experiences and to make the transition to a new period successfully."[2]

After forty years many survivors now face a transition point in their lives that has been accompanied by "a characteristic return of memories" about the Holocaust:

> For some . . . there is . . . the increasing awareness that life is not forever, and that one must remember before one ends one's journey. . . . For others . . . there [is] a reduction in the pattern of maximal activity that was used as a way of avoiding pain and mourning. The past now begins to emerge. It can become a resource or a menace. As an enduring repository of valuable memories, it can be drawn on and mobilized as a resource to maintain one's psychological equilibrium, or it can be a volcano that has long lain dormant and now spills forth its searing lava of memories, including delayed and neglected grief reactions. The reemergence of memory is a renewed challenge. The period of reconnection with the past can become a source for new creative activity . . . [and] new regard for the survivor, the continuity of Jewish life, and the meaningfulness of all human life.[3]

Clearly the Holocaust has become an increasingly central feature of Jewish consciousness. Yet some express concern that Jews have focused too much on their status as victims, as people who have suffered. David Vital writes:

> It is one thing to retain the memory of the Holocaust as an act of piety toward the dead and as a catastrophe . . . [that] deserve[s] to be studied and examined, not only for [its] own sake, but in the interests of finally reordering the life of the Jews as a people and as individuals. It is quite another to . . . [allow] . . . the Holocaust . . . to diminish all else in Judaism and Jewry and . . . permanently and compulsively fix our attention on the past . . . [and] make Jews a people of invalids, of victims, of death.[4]

Others Jews have echoed this sentiment and encouraged those who have strayed from the religious path to return to the practice of their faith. Jewish theologian Emil Fackenheim even sets forth a "614th Commandment" that commands Jews "to survive as Jews, lest the Jewish people perish" and that forbids Jews "to deny or despair of the God of Israel, lest Judaism perish." To do otherwise, according to Fackenheim, is to grant Hitler "yet other posthumous victories."[5]

But where does this dictum leave the survivors who, like my father, are not observant Jews?[6] Where does it leave those of the second and third generation who, like myself, are not observant Jews and who may have married (or will marry) outside of the faith? These are questions I will continue to examine in my own life. However, I believe that those of us who are born Jews remain Jews regardless of our religious beliefs. This is one thing that Hitler and the Nazis proved quite forcefully. Amos Funkenstein, professor of Jewish history, notes:

> All antisemitic ideologies since the end of the nineteenth century are directed less against traditional, orthodox Jews who can be recognized as Jews, and . . . more against Jews who are well acculturated and assimilated. . . . [They assume] that being Jewish is an unobliterable, indelible, innate character, [and that] the assimilated Jew deceives, in the best case, both himself [or herself] and others; or, in the worst case, his [or her] assimilation is a conspiratorial pretense whose purpose is to undermine the healthy texture of the society from within.[7]

But all must not be negative. For me there is an affirmative Jewish identity to be discovered through explorations of Jewish ethics and the vast heritage of Jewish intellectual, scientific, literary, and artistic achievement.[8] At the same time, I must continue to tell the story of the Holocaust. That story must be told, not simply because a past not remembered may be (is being) repeated,[9] but because through stories of the past, we construct ourselves.[10] Through stories of survival we gather strength and a sense of our potential as a people. If we tell these stories, our children will listen.

Michael visits the Duchowski family in Krosno (1989). *Left to right*, Mrs. Duch-owski, son Henryk, Michael, Mr. Duchowski.

Gate to Jewish cemetery in Krosno (1989).

Michael visits mass grave site where father is buried (1989).

Memorial stone at mass grave site (1989).

Michael visits Auschwitz I (1989).

Notes

PREFACE

1. Fogelman (1990).
2. Rosenbloom (1988, p. 158).
3. Anti-Defamation League (1993); Lipstadt (1993); Vidal-Naquet (1989, 1992).
4. Freeman (1991, p. 187); Markle et al. (1992).
5. Markle et al. (1992, p. 200).
6. Bauer (1990); Marrus (1987, 1991).
7. Davidson (1992, p. 24).

CHAPTER 1

1. Quoted in Schuman and Scott (1989, pp. 361–362); see also Halbachs (1980, 1992).
2. Schwartz (1991, p. 302); Halbachs (1980, 1992).
3. Epstein (1979); Fogelman (1990); Miller (1990).
4. Denzin (1989a, p. 82, 1970); Helling (1988); Thompson (1978).
5. Young (1988, p. 10). The term *Holocaust*, which has biblical origins, is somewhat of a misnomer since it suggests sacrifice to God. Moreover, if Germany had won the war, the Holocaust as such would not have existed but would have been described as something else — as solving the "Jewish problem" (Berger, 1993). Nevertheless, along with the Hebrew word *Shoah*, the term *Holocaust* retains meaning for Jews who remember the Nazi period as a "descent into almost indescribable cruelty" (Miller, 1990, p. 9).
6. Bauman (1989, pp. xiii).
7. The agency-structure problematic parallels but is distinct from other central concerns of social theory, including debates over micro- and macro-levels of analysis (Ritzer, 1992). Archer (1988, p. x) believes that an adequate representation of the relationship between agency and structure is the "acid test" of any general social theory. Symbolic interactionism is the branch of American social

theory that has focused most on the problem of "action" (Charon, 1992). However, Ritzer (1992) argues that a tradition of philosophical inquiry into the nature of agency (sometimes addressed as praxis or action) has played a greater role in the development of European theory (see Bernstein, 1971; Detmer, 1988). As the best examples of European theorizing on agency and structure, he offers Giddens (1984), Archer (1988), Bourdieu (1977), and Habermas (1987). Recently Sewell (1992) has addressed the agency-structure problematic as a central concern for American sociology. American sociologists have focused more than their European counterparts on questions regarding the relationship between micro- and macro-levels of analysis (Ritzer, 1992). They have examined the "microfoundations of macrosociology" (Collins, 1981) and the "macrofoundations of microsociology" (Fine, 1991). But the agency-structure issue has no direct connections to this concern since agency and structure are implicated at both levels of analysis (Ritzer, 1992).

8. Glaser and Strauss (1967).

9. Alexander (1982).

10. Mills (1959, p. 6); Denzin (1989a).

11. For instance, Giddens (1984) develops a theory of "structuration" and Archer (1988) a theory of "morphogenesis." Bourdieu (1977) focuses on the relationship between "habitus" and "field" and Habermas (1987) on the "colonization of the life-world." Sewell (1992), whose work derives from Giddens and Bourdieu, is primarily interested in the transformation of social structure. It is worth noting that Giddens (1979, 1984) is one of the few general social theorists who actually uses the Holocaust to advance some of his theoretical concepts. He draws on Bettelheim's (1960) analysis of human behavior in the concentration camps to illustrate the role of "routinization" — recurring social practices that constitute institutionalized social life — in establishing individuals' sense of identity and ontological security. Giddens (1984, p. 61) views the camp experience as a "critical situation," a "radical disjuncture of an unpredictable kind" that provides insight into routinized social life in instances where established modes of interaction have been undermined or destroyed. But here Giddens expresses a concern less with agency and more with Freudian notions of the unconscious. For instance, he views "critical situations" as occasions where "heightened anxiety renders actors vulnerable to regressive modes of object-affiliation involving a strong measure of ambivalence" (1979, p. 127). Moreover, whereas Giddens argues that agency is abandoned in "critical situations," I suggest that it often remains present and ongoing under such circumstances.

12. Denzin (1989b, p. 7).

13. Lifton (1980).

14. Des Pres (1976, pp. 7–8); Langer (1991, p. 199).

15. Sewell (1992, p. 20).

16. Blum et al. (1991); Des Pres (1976); Frankl (1959); Helmreich (1992); Langer (1991); Mack (1988); Rothchild (1981).

17. Des Pres (1976, p. 99).

18. Helmreich (1992, p. 275); Langer (1991).

19. Denzin (1989a, 1989b, p. 15).

20. Langer (1991, p. 151); Des Pres (1976); Dimsdale (1980); Hilberg (1992).

21. Sartre (1956, p. 457); Detmer (1988, p. 43). According to Sartre (1956, pp. 459, 483), resistance is a condition of freedom, for "there can be a free for-itself only as engaged in a resisting world. . . . The very project of freedom . . . implies the anticipation and acceptance of some kind of resistance."

22. Turner (1986, p. 41). Denzin (1991b, p. 62) argues that "the closest we ever get to 'raw' experience is when a subject is between interpretive worlds, experiencing a crisis, and is at a loss for an interpretive framework that would make sense of what he or she is experiencing."

23. Quoted in Schwartz (1991, p. 302).

24. Schuman and Scott (1989).

25. Gutman and Rozett (1990).

26. Hilberg (1991, p. 13).

27. Ibid. (p. 14); Markle et al. (1992). *Night* was originally published in a longer version in Yiddish as *And the World Was Silent*. *If This Be a Man* was later published as *Survival in Auschwitz*.

28. Friedlander (1992, p. 48); Helmreich (1992); Miller (1990).

29. Davidson (1992, pp. 14–15). More generally, Davidson (1992, pp. 149, 207) adds, survivor avoidance "is a universal human phenomenon, . . . for what they have to say disturbs our conception of man, and makes us feel uncomfortable and guilty. . . . The guilt is an extension of the guilt projected onto the survivor for not having actively intervened to help the victims and [is] derived from fears of the possibility of experiencing the same fate. . . . [The survivor] is a disturber of the peace, . . . a 'messenger of evil tidings'. . . [who] represents the possibility of chaos and disintegration of society. . . . Worst of all, survivors of a calamity can even arouse a feeling of contamination, as if being in contact with their confrontation with death could be contagious."

30. Ibid.

31. Ibid. (p. 20). See Segev (1993) and Young (1993) for discussions of how this view is manifested in Israeli political and memorial culture. For example, the Yad Vashem Museum is designated as "The Memorial Authority of the Holocaust and Heroism."

32. Segev (1993).

33. Eichmann's prosecutor, Attorney General Gideon Hausner, wanted to "bring before the entire world the hundreds and thousands of heroic deeds that were not generally known" (quoted in Segev, 1993, p. 353). Both Jews and non-Jews were to be reminded that Israel was the only country in the world that could guarantee Jewish security and that the nation was ready and able to defend itself.

34. Schmitt (1989, p. 247).

35. Miller (1990, p. 223).

36. Gitlin (1983). In West Germany the Holocaust docudrama even helped mobilize public support for an extension of the statute of limitations on atrocity crimes.

37. Miller (1990, pp. 231, 225).

38. Quoted in Ibid. (p. 220).

39. Arendt (1963); Hilberg (1985); Rubenstein and Roth (1987, p. 160).

40. Bettelheim (1960).

41. Dimsdale (1980); Marrus (1987).

42. Helmreich (1992, p. 14); see also Chodoff (1980); Davidson (1992); Eitinger (1980).

43. Des Pres (1976).

44. Ibid. (p. 99); Pawełcyńska (1979, p. 144); Gallant and Cross (1992); Davidson (1992, p. 121). Also see Benner et al. (1980); Dimsdale (1980); Frankl (1959); Luchterhand (1967); Pingel (1991); Unger (1986).

45. Des Pres (1976, p. 201); Frankl (1959, pp. 86–87); Unger (1986); Botz (1991); Helmreich (1992, pp. 111, 276).

46. Langer (1991, p. 109, 1993). Langer (1991, p. 163) cites Gilbert (1985, p. 828) as an example of such romanticism.

47. Langer (1991, pp. 180, 183).

48. Benner et al. (1980, pp. 219, 235, 236, 238).

49. Giddens (1976, 1979, 1984); Sewell (1992).

50. Denzin (1989a, 1989b, 1989c); Gallant and Cross (1992); Glaser and Strauss (1964, 1971); Goffman (1959, 1961); Schmitt (1989).

51. Sewell (1992, p. 21).

52. Denzin (1989c, p. 5).

53. Gallant and Cross (1992, p. 235).

54. Alexander (1984, p. 5, 1988); Reynolds (1993).

55. Sewell (1992, pp. 4, 20). Borrowing a term from Bourdieu (1977), Sewell (1992, p. 17) argues that cultural schemas and resources are "transposable," that is, "they can be applied in a wide and not fully predictable range of cases outside the context in which they are initially learned."

56. Berger (1993); Hilberg (1985).

57. Hilberg (1992, pp. 159, 188).

58. Sewell (1992, p. 21).

59. Des Pres (1976); Pawełczyńska (1979).

60. Oliner and Oliner (1988); Tec (1986).

61. Giddens (1984).

62. Denzin (1989c, p. 5).

63. Sartre (1956, pp. 480, 483).

64. Helling (1988, pp. 222–223).

65. Blum et al. (1991); Robinson (1986).

66. Denzin (1989b, p. 17).

67. Ibid; Brewer (1986).

68. Langer (1991, p. xv).

69. President Reagan accepted an invitation from Chancellor Helmut Kohl of West Germany to attend a commemorative ceremony at a German military cemetery in Bitburg, which was the burial site of about two thousand German soldiers as well as nearly fifty Nazi SS men (Hartman, 1986; Schmitt, 1989).

   Michael also recalls with anger President John Kennedy's 1962 visit to Germany, where he declared, "*Ich bin ein Berliner*." But I believe the most important emotional reminder in the brothers' case is the state of Israel itself and the threat they perceive to its well-being. Important as well is their awareness of those who deny that the Holocaust occurred (Anti-Defamation League, 1993; Lipstadt, 1993; Vidal-Naquet, 1989, 1992).

70. Levi (1961); Frankel (1991); Nahon (1989); Wiesel (1960).

71. These interviews were conducted in the spring of 1989 on a trip to Poland. I traveled with Michael, who still speaks Polish and served as a translator.

72. See especially Gutman (1990).

73. Young (1988, pp. 25, 33).

74. Hartman (1988, p. 1714).

75. Frankl (1959); Levi (1961); Wiesel (1960).

76. Blumer (1969).

77. Gutman and Rozett (1990).

78. Denzin (1970, p. 243).

79. Levin (1986, p. 92).

80. Friedlander (1992, p. 51); Gallant and Cross (1992). Denzin (1989a, p. 83) reminds us "that our primary obligation is always to the people we study, not to our project . . . or discipline. . . . [Their] lives and stories . . . are given to us under a promise . . . that we protect those who have shared with us."

81. Langer (1991, p. 22). ⟨

82. Young (1988, p. 39).

83. Helmreich (1992). Davidson (1992, p. 22) notes that "in the life cycle of individuals who experienced the Holocaust, the passage of forty years enabled many . . . to arrive at a degree of emotional distance that allowed a greater recalling of traumatic memories without the agonizing pain that a time closer to the events brought [forth]."

84. Miller (1990, p. 268).

85. Blum et al. (1991); Davidson (1992).

86. For a discussion of similar reactions from Jews in the United States and Israel, see Davidson (1992); Helmreich (1992); Segev (1993). Michael added that "it was a little different with the non-Jewish people who didn't know as much [as the Jews] about what happened. I felt that they were actually more interested to hear about it."

87. Blauner (1987, p. 54).

88. This strategy is followed by Blauner (1987); Coles (1975); and Helmreich (1992).

89. Denzin (1989a, p. 189).

CHAPTER 2

1. Gutman (1990a); Gutman and Rozett (1990).

2. For more detailed discussions of Jews in Polish history, see Gutman (1990a); Fuks et al. (1982); Hertz (1988); Heller (1977); Kagan (1992); Lukas (1986); Paldiel (1993); Tec (1986).

3. Rubenstein and Roth (1987).

4. Gutman (1990a, p. 1153).

5. Paldiel (1993, p. 178).

6. Tec (1986, p. 14).

7. Kagan (1992).

8. Helena died before the outbreak of World War II.

9. Helmreich (1992).

10. Oliner and Oliner (1988); Tec (1986).

11. Tec (1986).

12. Goffman (1959).

13. Tec (1986).

14. Ibid.; Paldiel (1993).

15. Gallant and Cross (1992); Rothchild (1981); Wiesel (1960).

16. For discussions of Jewish youth movements in Europe, see Gutman (1990b).

17. Caplan (1993, p. 222).

18. Glaser and Strauss (1971, pp. 2, 89).

19. Rothchild (1981, p. 9).

20. Prior to the invasion of Poland, emigration, not extermination, had been the focus of Nazi efforts to remove Jews from the Third Reich. However, the conquest of Poland, with its large Jewish population, made expulsion from German-occupied territories more difficult to accomplish. Similar problems accrued as the Nazis expanded their influence in western Europe. Nevertheless, as late as the summer of 1940 the Nazis were evaluating various proposals to deport European Jews to the French colony of Madagascar, an island off the coast of southeastern Africa. But they were unable to work out the details, as the German Foreign Office and the SS clashed on specifics and as Germany's faltering air campaign against the British preoccupied Nazi officials (Berger, 1993; Browning, 1978, 1989; Marrus, 1987).

The definitive decision to exterminate all European Jews does not seem to have occurred until after the German attack on the Soviet Union in June 1941. Although Hitler appears to have given an oral directive, he never issued a written order for the "final solution" (Bauer, 1991). Rather, at the end of July 1941 Reinhard Heydrich, head of the Reich Security Main Office, received written orders from Hermann Göring, Hitler's chief deputy, to "make all the preparations in organizational, practical, and material matters for a total solution of the Jewish question in territories under German influence" and to submit a master plan "in the near future" (cited in Schleunes, 1970, p. 175). Hilberg characterizes Göring's directive as an "authorization to invent . . . something that was not as yet capable of being put into words" (interview in Lanzmann, 1985, pp. 72–73). In January 1942 the directive to work out the details of a plan was officially transmitted to a group of high-ranking Nazi functionaries at the infamous Wannsee Conference.

CHAPTER 3

1. Deportations of Jews from Łódź to other parts of Poland began in November 1939 (Krakowski, 1990b).

2. Gilbert (1982) estimates that about five thousand Jews were liquidated in Krosno and the surrounding areas in August 1942.

3. Gallant and Cross (1992).

4. For a brief discussion of Organisation Todt, see Wilhelm (1990).

CHAPTER 4

1. Mrs. Duchowski recollects that Shlomo asked her for help.

2. Oliner and Oliner (1988); Tec (1986).

3. Glaser and Strauss (1964, p. 670).

4. Oliner and Oliner (1988); Tec (1986).

5. The Germans began occupying Czortków on July 6, 1941. Four days later the Ukrainians, with the help of the Germans, staged a pogrom against the Jewish population, killing about three hundred Jews (Weiss, 1990).

6. Tec (1990).

7. For discussions of Jews in the Partisan movement, see Bauer (1989); Gutman (1990b); Rubenstein and Roth (1987); Tec (1990, 1993); Werner (1992).

8. NKVD stood for the State Security Committee, or People's Commissariat of Internal Affairs. It later became the KGB.

LIVERPOOL
JOHN MOORES UNIVERSITY
TRUEMAN STREET LIBRARY
TEL. 051 231 4022/4023

Chapter 5

1. Michael did not want the name of this relative to appear in the book.
2. Krakowski (1990c).
3. Ibid. The Szebnie camp is now a school; only a plaque serves to remind people of what transpired there.
4. Buszko (1990); Nahon (1989).
5. Unger (1986).
6. Levine is a pseudonym.
7. Nahon (1989).
8. Unger (1986, pp. 287, 290); Gallant and Cross (1992).
9. Goffman (1961, pp. 188–189).
10. Des Pres (1976, p. 108).
11. Benner et al. (1980); Pingel (1991).
12. For a discussion of IG Farben and its relationship to the Third Reich, see Hayes (1987). The term Buna refers to the rubber factory that was being built at this location.
13. Bettelheim (1960).
14. Gallant and Cross (1992, p. 238); Pawełczyńska (1979).
15. Michael added, "After my liberation, I met this man in Munich. He seemed pleased to see me alive. I, however, did not feel the same about him."
16. Pingel (1991).
17. Langer (1991, p. 124).
18. See Tec (1986) on the practice of collective punishment outside of the camps in Poland.
19. For discussions of resistance in the concentration camps, see Bauer (1989); Gutman and Saf (1984); Müller (1979); Pawełcyńska (1979).
20. See Wyman (1984) for a discussion of the bombing controversy.

Chapter 6

1. The evacuation occurred on January 18 (Levi, 1961).
2. Ibid.; Buszko (1990).
3. Krakowski (1990a); Marrus (1987).
4. Pingel (1990).
5. Helmreich (1992).
6. Leichter (1990).
7. Bauer (1970).
8. Later Gusta learned that she did have relatives who had survived.

9. Bauer (1970).

10. Helmreich (1992); Segev (1993).

11. After the war the displaced persons camps had the highest birth rate of any Jewish community in the world (Helmreich, 1992).

CHAPTER 7

1. Freeman (1991); Markle et al. (1992); Rittner (1990); Rosenfeld and Green-berg (1978).

2. Sachar (1992, pp. 848–849).

3. Ibid.

4. Quoted in Markle et al. (1992, p. 200).

5. Bauer (1990, p. 147); Marrus (1987, 1991).

6. Markle et al. (1992, pp. 180, 200).

7. Friedlander (1992, p. 52).

8. Hilberg (1985, p. 300); Johnson (1987); Rubenstein and Roth (1987).

9. Frankl (1959, pp. 103–104; my emphasis).

10. Prior to the war the United States actually turned away from its ports Jews who were fleeing Nazi persecution. Moreover, the Allies did not fight World War II to liberate the Jews but to protect their own status as independent and free nations. They did not divert even one bomb to eliminate the gas chambers or the railway lines that led Jews to their deaths (Breitman and Kraut, 1987; Rubenstein and Roth, 1987; Simpson, 1993; Wyman, 1984).

11. Langer (1991, p. 157).

12. Caplan (1993, p. 224).

13. Hartman (1986, p. 2).

14. Roiphe (1988, p. 16).

15. Chodoff (1980); Davidson (1992); Eitinger (1980).

16. Davidson (1992, p. 145).

17. Ibid.

18. Helmreich (1992).

19. Ryan (1971); Wright (1993).

20. Amato (1990, p. 212).

21. Ibid.; Maier (1988); Marrus (1991); Sykes (1992).

22. Dworkin (1979); Firestone (1970, p. 1).

23. Kaminer (1993); Sykes (1992).

24. Quoted in Amato (1990, pp. 159–160; my emphasis). Akbar is a former president of the National Association of Black Psychologists.

25. Kaminer (1993, p. 31).

26. Marrus (1991, p. 111); Segev (1993); Young (1993).

27. Marrus (1991, pp. 112, 116); Neusner (1981, p. 90).

28. Roiphe (1988, p. 163).

29. Vidal-Naquet (1989, p. 317); Marrus (1991); Segev (1993).

30. Marrus (1991, p. 114).

31. Marcus (1993).

32. Quoted in Anti-Defamation League (1993, p. 3); also see Marrus (1991).

33. Roiphe (1988, pp. 166, 170).

34. ADL (1993, p. 1).

35. Quoted in Marrus (1991, p. 110). Friedlander (1984) believes that the numerous representations of fascism and the Holocaust in popular fiction and film have actually served to trivialize the events of the Nazi period rather than enlighten the public.

36. Marrus (1991, pp. 109–110).

37. ADL (1993, p. 1).

38. Alter (1993, p. 117). There has been controversy over the wording of the question in this Roper poll, which contained a double negative: "Does it seem possible or does it seem impossible to you that the Nazi extermination of the Jews never happened?" In a January 1994 Gallup poll that asked, "Do you doubt that the Holocaust actually happened, or not?," only 13 percent expressed doubt or were unsure. When Gallup asked, "Just to clarify, in your opinion, did the Holocaust definitely happen, probably happen, probably not happen, or definitely not happen?," 19 percent said probably not or definitely not (Associated Press story reported in "Survey," *Rocky Mountain News*, 1994).

39. ADL (1993, p. 2).

40. There is a rapidly expanding literature on this topic. See Baldwin (1990); Bartov (1993); Evans (1989); Friedlander, ed. (1992); Friedlander (1993); Hartman (1986); Maier (1988); Markle and McCrea (1990); Miller (1990); Santner (1990).

41. Knowlton and Cates (1993); Nolte (1965).

42. Hartman (1986, p. 5). See Young (1993) for an insightful study of national variations in Holocaust memorial culture in Germany, Poland, Israel, and the United States. Markle and McCrea (1990, pp. 144, 146) suggest that the relationship between past and present in different countries is an "interactive and interpretative" process whereby the past is constructed "to legitimize the present and promote a desired future" for the nation.

43. ADL (1993); Lipstadt (1993); Vidal-Naquet (1989, 1992).

44. Quoted in Miller (1990, p. 220).

45. Quoted in Roiphe (1988, p. 165).

46. Bartov (1993).

47. See Denzin (1991a); Gottdiener (1993); Katovich and MacMurray (1991); Rosenau (1992). A distinction can be made between postmodernity as a state of contemporary society and postmodernism as a mode of social criticism or

as an epistemological position. In regard to the former, the ambiguous memory of the Holocaust itself is to some extent characteristic of the historical amnesia that is inherent in postmodern culture (Huyssen, 1993). In regard to the latter, critics of postmodern thought contend that it provides no basis for making moral judgments and hence tends toward "relativism or radical indeterminancy, which, at best, results in passive, status quo politics and, at worst, fails to defend against fascism and terrorism" (Handler, 1992, p. 698; Harvey, 1989).

48. Musolf (1993, pp. 232–233).

49. Bartov (1993, pp. 112, 114).

50. Quoted in Remak (1969, p. 154; my emphasis).

51. Quoted in Bartov (1993, p. 110).

52. Bartov (1993, pp. 113–114).

53. Katovich and MacMurray (1991, p. 77).

54. Funkenstein (1992).

55. Bartov (1993, p. 113).

56. Johnson and Altheide (1991, p. 54); Alexander (1990).

57. Hartman (1993, p. 245).

58. Schwartz (1991).

59. Thanks to the Holocaust survivor videotape projects at Yale University, UCLA, and other research centers, future generations will be able to *see* the survivors tell their stories (Blum et al., 1991; Hartman, 1988; Langer, 1991; Young, 1988).

60. Denzin (1989a, p. 83).

61. Quoted in Rothchild (1981, p. 10).

EPILOGUE

1. Siegal is a pseudonym.

2. Davidson (1992, p. 22).

3. Ibid.

4. Vital (1991, pp. 137–138).

5. Fackenheim (1978), cited in Rubenstein and Roth (1987, p. 319) and Sachar (1992, p. 851). In traditional Judaism God is said to have given Israel in scripture 613 commandments.

6. Brenner (1980).

7. Funkenstein (1992, p. 76).

8. Sachar (1992).

9. At the time of this writing, the so-called ethnic cleansing campaign in the former Yugoslavia has reached genocidal proportions (Walker, 1993). Even

though the Holocaust will forever retain its particularistic meaning for Jews, its universalistic implications cannot be ignored. Otherwise, we are all left vulnerable to not knowing "whether we have been, are, or will be a party to something similar" (Porpora, 1990, p. 4). Bartov (1993, p. 103) suggests that notable Holocaust author-survivors such as Jean Amery and Primo Levi may have ultimately fallen to despair, not because of difficulties overcoming their own personal suffering, but because of their realization that Auschwitz was not the end but rather "the beginning of a new age."

10. Amato (1990); Denzin (1989a); Rosenwald and Ochberg (1992).

References

SOURCES ON JEWS AND THE HOLOCAUST

Alter, Jonathan. 1993. "After the Survivors." *Newsweek* (December 20):117–118, 120.

Anti-Defamation League (ADL). 1993. *Hitler's Apologists: The Anti-Semitic Propaganda of Holocaust "Revisionism."* New York: Anti-Defamation League.

Arendt, Hannah. 1963. *Eichmann in Jerusalem: A Report on the Banality of Evil.* New York: Viking Press.

Baldwin, Peter (ed.). 1990. *Reworking the Past: Hitler, the Holocaust, and the Historians' Debate.* Boston: Beacon Press.

Bartov, Omer. 1993. "Intellectuals on Auschwitz: Memory, History, and Truth." *History and Memory: Studies in Representation of the Past* 5:87–129.

Bauer, Yehuda. 1970. *Bricha: Flight and Rescue.* New York: Random House.

———. 1989. "Jewish Resistance and Passivity in the Face of the Holocaust." Pp. 235–251 in F. Furet (ed.), *Unanswered Questions: Nazi Germany and the Genocide of the Jews.* New York: Schocken.

———. 1990. "Is the Holocaust Explicable?" *Holocaust and Genocide Studies* 5: 145–155.

———. 1991. "Who Was Responsible and When? Some Well-Known Documents Revisited." *Holocaust and Genocide Studies* 6:129–149.

Bauman, Zygmunt. 1989. *Modernity and the Holocaust.* Ithaca, N.Y.: Cornell University Press.

Benner, Patricia, Ethel Roskies, and Richard S. Lazarus. 1980. "Stress and Coping Under Extreme Conditions." Pp. 219–258 in J. Dimsdale (ed.), *Survivors, Victims, and Perpetrators: Essays on the Nazi Holocaust.* New York: Hemisphere.

Berger, Ronald J. 1993. "The 'Banality of Evil' Reframed: The Social Construction of the 'Final Solution' to the 'Jewish Problem.'" *The Sociological Quarterly* 34:597–618.

Bettleheim, Bruno. 1960. *The Informed Heart.* Glencoe, Ill.: Free Press.

Blum, Lenore et al. (Holocaust Educational Foundation Volunteers). 1991. "Tellers and Listeners: The Impact of Holocaust Narratives." Pp. 316–328 in P. Hayes (ed.), *Lessons and Legacies: The Meaning of the Holocaust in a Changing World*. Evanston, Ill.: Northwestern University Press.

Botz, Gerhard (ed.). 1991. *I Want to Speak: The Tragedy and Banality of Survival in Terezin and Auschwitz*, by Margareta Glas-Larsson. Riverside, Calif.: Ariadne Press.

Breitman, Richard, and Alan M. Kraut. 1987. *American Refugee Policy and European Jewry, 1933–1945*. Bloomington: Indiana University Press.

Brenner, Reeve Robert. 1980. *The Faith and Doubt of Holocaust Survivors*. New York: Free Press.

Browning, Christopher R. 1978. *The Final Solution and the German Foreign Office*. New York: Holmes and Meier.

————. 1989. "The Decision Concerning the Final Solution." Pp. 96–118 in F. Furet (ed.), *Unanswered Questions: Nazi Germany and the Genocide of the Jews*. New York: Schocken.

Buszko, Jozef. 1990. "Auschwitz." Pp. 107–119 in I. Gutman (ed.), *Encyclopedia of the Holocaust*. Vol. 1. New York: Macmillan.

Caplan, Sophie. 1993. "Polish and German Anti-Semitism." Pp. 221–240 in J. Milfull (ed.), *Why Germany? National Socialist Anti-Semitism and the European Context*. Oxford: Berg.

Chodoff, Paul. 1980. "Psychotherapy of the Survivor." Pp. 205–218 in J. Dimsdale (ed.), *Survivors, Victims, and Perpetrators: Essays on the Nazi Holocaust*. New York: Hemisphere.

Davidson, Shamai. 1992. *Holding on to Humanity — the Message of Holocaust Survivors: The Shamai Davidson Papers*. Edited by I. Charny. New York: New York University Press.

Des Pres, Terrence. 1976. *The Survivor: An Anatomy of Life in the Death Camps*. New York: Oxford University Press.

Dimsdale, Joel E. 1980. "The Coping Behavior of Nazi Concentration Camp Survivors." Pp. 163–174 in J. Dimsdale (ed.), *Survivors, Victims, and Perpetrators: Essays on the Nazi Holocaust*. New York: Hemisphere.

Eitinger, Leo. 1980. "The Concentration Camp Syndrome and Its Late Sequelae." Pp. 127–162 in J. Dimsdale (ed.), *Survivors, Victims, and Perpetrators: Essays on the Nazi Holocaust*. New York: Hemisphere.

Epstein, Helen. 1979. *Children of the Holocaust: Conversations with Sons and Daughters of Survivors*. New York: Penguin.

Evans, Richard J. 1989. *In Hitler's Shadow: West German Historians and the Attempt to Escape from the Nazi Past*. New York: Pantheon.

Fackenheim, Emil L. 1978. *The Jewish Return into History: Reflections in the Age of Auschwitz and a New Jerusalem*. New York: Schocken.

Fogelman, Eva. 1990. "Second Generation of Survivors." Pp. 1434–1435 in I. Gutman (ed.), *Encyclopedia of the Holocaust*. Vol. 3. New York: Macmillan.

Frankel, Neftali. 1991. *I Survived Hell: The Testimony of a Survivor of the Nazi Extermination Camps*. New York: Vantage.

Frankl, Viktor E. 1959. *Man's Search for Meaning*. Rev. ed. New York: Pocket Books.

Freeman, Michael. 1991. "The Theory and Prevention of Genocide." *Holocaust and Genocide Studies* 6:185–199.

Friedlander, Saul. 1984. *Reflections of Nazism: An Essay on Kitsch and Death*. New York: Harper and Row.

———. 1992. "Trauma, Transference, and 'Working Through' in Writing the History of the Shoah." *History and Memory: Studies in Representation of the Past* 4:39–59.

———. 1993. *Memory, History, and the Extermination of the Jews of Europe*. Bloomington: Indiana University Press.

———. (ed). 1992. *Probing the Limits of Representation: Nazism and the "Final Solution."* Cambridge, Mass.: Harvard University Press.

Fuks, Marian, Zygmunt Hoffman, Maurycy Horn, and Jerzy Tomaszewski. 1982. *Polish Jewry: History and Culture*. Warsaw: Interpress.

Funkenstein, Amos. 1992. "History, Counterhistory, and Narrative." Pp. 66–81 in S. Friedlander (ed.), *Probing the Limits of Representation: Nazism and the "Final Solution."* Cambridge, Mass.: Harvard University Press.

Gallant, Mary J., and Jay E. Cross. 1992. "Surviving Destruction of the Self: Challenged Identity in the Holocaust." Pp. 221–246 in N. Denzin (ed.), *Studies in Symbolic Interaction*. Vol. 13. Greenwich, Conn.: JAI Press.

Gilbert, Martin. 1982. *The Macmillan Atlas of the Holocaust*. New York: Macmillan.

———. 1985. *The Holocaust: A History of the Jews of Europe During the Second World War*. New York: Holt, Rinehart and Winston.

Gitlin, Todd. 1983. "Movies of the Week." Pp. 157–200 in T. Gitlin, *Inside Prime Time*. New York: Pantheon.

Gutman, Israel. 1990a. "The Jews in Poland." Pp. 1151–1176 in I. Gutman (ed.), *Encyclopedia of the Holocaust*. Vol. 3. New York: Macmillan.

———. 1990b. "Partisans." Pp. 1108–1122 in I. Gutman (ed.), *Encyclopedia of the Holocaust*. Vol. 3. New York: Macmillan.

———. (ed.). 1990. *Encyclopedia of the Holocaust*. New York: Macmillan.

Gutman, Israel, and Robert Rozett. 1990. "Estimated Jewish Losses in the Holocaust." Pp. 1797–1802 in I. Gutman (ed.), *Encyclopedia of the Holocaust*. Vol. 4. New York: Macmillan.

Gutman, Israel, and Avital Saf (eds.). 1984. *The Nazi Concentration Camps*. Jerusalem: Yad Vashem.

Hartman, Geoffrey. 1988. "Learning from Survivors: Notes on the Video Archive at Yale." Pp. 1713–1716 in *Remembering the Future*. Vol. 2, *The Impact of the Holocaust on the Contemporary World*. Oxford: Pergamon Press.

———. 1993. "Public Memory and Modern Experience." *Yale Journal of Criticism* 6:239–247.

———. (ed.). 1986. *Bitburg in Moral and Political Perspective*. Bloomington: Indiana University Press.

Hayes, Peter. 1987. *Industry and Ideology: IG Farben in the Nazi Era*. Cambridge: Cambridge University Press.

Heller, Celia S. 1977. *On the Edge of Destruction*. New York: Columbia University Press.

Helmreich, William B. 1992. *Against All Odds: Holocaust Survivors and the Successful Lives They Made in America*. New York: Simon and Schuster.

Hertz, Aleksander. 1988. *The Jews in Polish Culture*. Evanston, Ill.: Northwestern University Press.

Hilberg, Raul. 1985. *The Destruction of the European Jews*. Rev. ed. New York: Holmes and Meier.

———. 1991. "Opening Remarks: The Discovery of the Holocaust." Pp. 11–19 in P. Hayes (ed.), *Lessons and Legacies: The Meaning of the Holocaust in a Changing World*. Evanston, Ill.: Northwestern University Press.

———. 1992. *Perpetrators, Victims, Bystanders: The Jewish Catastrophe, 1933–1945*. New York: HarperCollins.

Huyssen, Andreas. 1993. "Monument and Memory in a Postmodern Age." *Yale Journal of Criticism* 6:249–261.

Johnson, Paul. 1987. *A History of the Jews*. New York: Harper and Row.

Kagan, Joram. 1992. *Poland's Jewish Heritage*. New York: Hippocrene.

Knowlton, James, and Truett Cates (trans.). 1993. *Forever in the Shadow of Hitler?* Atlantic Highlands, N.J.: Humanities Press.

Krakowski, Shmuel. 1990a. "Death Marches." Pp. 349–354 in I. Gutman (ed.), *Encyclopedia of the Holocaust*. Vol. 1. New York: Macmillan.

———. 1990b. "Łódź." Pp. 900–909 in I. Gutman (ed.), *Encyclopedia of the Holocaust*. Vol. 3. New York: Macmillan.

———. 1990c. "Rzeszów." Pp. 1314–1317 in I. Gutman (ed.), *Encyclopedia of the Holocaust*. Vol. 3. New York: Macmillan.

Langer, Lawrence L. 1991. *Holocaust Testimonies: The Ruins of Memory*. New Haven, Conn.: Yale University Press.

———. 1993. "A Tainted Legacy: Remembering the Warsaw Ghetto." *Tikkun: A Bimonthly Jewish Critique of Politics, Culture, and Society* 8 (May–June): 37–40, 85–87.

Lanzmann, Claude. 1985. *Shoah: An Oral History of the Holocaust*. New York: Pantheon.

Leichter, Sinai. 1990. "Kielce." Pp. 800–803 in I. Gutman (ed.), *Encyclopedia of the Holocaust*. Vol. 2. New York: Macmillan.

Levi, Primo. 1961. *Survival in Auschwitz*. New York: Collier.

Levin, Nora. 1986. "Some Reservations About Lanzmann's Shoah." *Sh'ma: A Journal of Jewish Responsiblity* (April 18):89–93.

Lifton, Robert J. 1980. "The Concept of the Survivor." Pp. 113–126 in J. Dimsdale (ed.), *Survivors, Victims, and Perpetrators: Essays on the Nazi Holocaust*. New York: Hemisphere.

Lipstadt, Deborah E. 1993. *Denying the Holocaust: The Growing Assault on Truth and Memory*. New York: Free Press.

Luchterhand, Elmer. 1967. "Prisoner Behaviour and Social System in the Nazi Concentration Camp." *International Journal of Psychiatry* 13:245–264.

Lukas, Richard C. 1986. *Forgotten Holocaust: The Poles Under German Occupation 1939–1944.* Lexington: University Press of Kentucky.

Mack, John E., with Rita S. Rogers. 1988. *The Alchemy of Survival: One Woman's Journey.* Reading, Mass.: Addison-Wesley.

Maier, Charles S. 1988. *The Unmasterable Past: History, Holocaust, and German National Identity.* Cambridge, Mass.: Harvard University Press.

Marcus, Amy Dockser. 1993. "Turning a Page: As Holocaust Memory Fades, Israel Faces Difficult Transition." *Wall Street Journal* (March 31): A1, A6.

Markle, Gerald E., Mary D. Lagerwey-Voorman, Todd A. Clason, Jill A. Green, and Tricia L. Meade. 1992. "From Auschwitz to Americana: Texts of the Holocaust." *Sociological Focus* 25:179–202.

Markle, Gerald E., and Frances B. McCrea. 1990. "Forgetting and Remembering: Bitburg and the Social Construction of History." Pp. 143–159 in G. Miller and J. Holstein (eds.), *Perspectives on Social Problems.* Vol. 2. Greenwich, Conn.: JAI Press.

Marrus, Michael. 1987. *The Holocaust in History.* New York: New American Library.

———. 1991. "The Use and Misuse of the Holocaust." Pp. 106–119 in P. Hayes (ed.), *Lessons and Legacies: The Meaning of the Holocaust in a Changing World.* Evanston, Ill.: Northwestern University Press.

Miller, Judith. 1990. *One, by One, by One: Facing the Holocaust.* New York: Touchstone.

Müller, Filip. 1979. *Eyewitness Auschwitz: Three Years in the Gas Chambers.* New York: Stein and Day.

Nahon, Marco. 1989. *Birkenau: The Camp of Death.* Tuscaloosa: University of Alabama Press.

Neusner, Jacob. 1981. *Stranger at Home: "The Holocaust," Zionism, and American Judaism.* Chicago: University of Chicago Press.

Nolte, Ernst. 1965. *Three Faces of Fascism.* New York: Holt, Rinehart and Winston.

Oliner, Samuel P., and Pearl M. Oliner. 1988. *The Altruistic Personality: Rescuers of Jews in Nazi Europe.* New York: Free Press.

Paldiel, Mordecai. 1993. "Poland." Pp. 176–236 in M. Paldiel, *The Path of the Righteous: Gentile Rescuers of Jews During the Holocaust.* Hoboken, N.J.: KTAV.

Paweɬczyńska, Anna. 1979. *Values and Violence in Auschwitz: A Sociological Analysis.* Berkeley and Los Angeles: University of California Press.

Pingel, Falk. 1990. "Natzweiler-Struthof." Pp. 1037–1038 in I. Gutman (ed.), *Encyclopedia of the Holocaust.* Vol. 3. New York: Macmillan.

———. 1991. "The Destruction of Human Identity in Concentration Camps: The Contribution of the Social Sciences to an Analysis of Behavior Under Extreme Conditions." *Holocaust and Genocide Studies* 6:167–184.

Porpora, Douglas V. 1990. *How Holocausts Happen: The United States in Central America.* Philadelphia: Temple University Press.

Remak, Joachim (ed.). 1969. *The Nazi Years: A Documentary History.* Englewood Cliffs, N.J.: Prentice-Hall.

Rittner, Carol. 1990. *Elie Wiesel: Between Memory and Hope.* New York: New York University Press.

Roiphe, Anne. 1988. *A Season for Healing: Reflections on the Holocaust.* New York: Summit.

Rosenbloom, Maria. 1988. "Lessons of the Holocaust for Mental Health Practice." Pp. 145–159 in R. Braham (ed.), *Psychological Perspectives on the Holocaust.* New York: Columbia University Press.

Rosenfeld, Alvin H., and Irving Greenberg (eds.). 1978. *Confronting the Holocaust: The Impact of Elie Wiesel.* Bloomington: Indiana University Press.

Rothschild, Sylvia (ed.). 1981. *Voices from the Holocaust.* New York: New American Library.

Rubenstein, Richard L., and John K. Roth. 1987. *Approaches to Auschwitz: The Holocaust and Its Legacy.* Atlanta: John Knox.

Sachar, Howard M. 1992. *A History of the Jews in America.* New York: Vintage.

Santner, Eric L. 1990. "On the Difficulty of Saying 'We': The 'Historians' Debate' and Edgard Reitz's Heimat." *History and Memory: Studies in Representation of the Past* 2:276–296.

Schluenes, Karl A. 1970. *The Twisted Road to Auschwitz: Nazi Policy Toward German Jews, 1933–1939.* Urbana: University of Illinois Press.

Schmitt, Raymond L. 1989. "Sharing the Holocaust: Bitburg as Emotional Reminder." Pp. 238–298 in N. Denzin (ed.), *Studies in Symbolic Interaction.* Vol. 10. Greenwich, Conn.: JAI Press.

Segev, Tom. 1993. *The Seventh Million: The Israelis and the Holocaust.* New York: Hill and Wang.

Simpson, Christopher. 1993. *The Splendid Blond Beast: Money, Law, and Genocide in the Twentieth Century.* New York: Grove Press."

"Survey on Holocaust Wrong." 1994. *Rocky Mountain News,* May 19, p. 43A.

Tec, Nechama. 1986. *When Light Pierced the Darkness: Christian Rescue of Jews in Nazi-Occupied Poland.* New York: Oxford University Press.

———. 1990. *In the Lion's Den: The Life of Oswald Rufeisen.* New York: Oxford University Press.

———. 1993. *Defiance: The Bielski Partisans.* New York: Oxford University Press.

Unger, Michael. 1986. "The Prisoner's First Encounter with Auschwitz." *Holocaust and Genocide Studies* 1:279–295.

Vidal-Naquet, Pierre. 1989. "Theses on Revisionism." Pp. 304–319 in F. Furet (ed.), *Unanswered Questions: Nazi Germany and the Genocide of the Jews.* New York: Schocken.

————. 1992. *Assassins of Memory: Essays on the Denial of the Holocaust*. New York: Columbia University Press.

Vital, David. 1991. "After the Catastrophe: Aspects of Contemporary Jewry." Pp. 120–138 in P. Hayes (ed.), *Lessons and Legacies: The Meaning of the Holocaust in a Changing World*. Evanston, Ill.: Northwestern University Press.

Walker, Stephen S. 1993. "Genocide: We Are Responsible." *Tikkun: A Bimonthly Jewish Critique of Politics, Culture, and Society* 8 (November–December): 19–22.

Weiss, Aharon. 1990. "Chortkov." Pp. 290–291 in I. Gutman (ed.), *Encyclopedia of the Holocaust*. Vol. 1. New York: Macmillan.

Werner, Harold. 1992. *Fighting Back: A Memoir of Jewish Resistance in World War II*. New York: Columbia University Press.

Wiesel, Elie. 1960. *Night*. New York: Bantam.

Wilhelm, Hans-Heinrich. 1990. "Organisation Todt." Pp. 1095–1096 in I. Gutman (ed.), *Encyclopedia of the Holocaust*. Vol. 3. New York: Macmillan.

Wyman, David S. 1984. *The Abandonment of the Jews: America and the Holocaust, 1941–1945*. New York: Pantheon.

Young, James. 1988. *Writing and Rewriting the Holocaust*. Indianapolis: Indiana University Press.

————. 1993. *The Texture of Memory: Holocaust Memorials and Meaning in Europe, Israel, and America*. New Haven, Conn.: Yale University Press.

SOURCES ON SOCIAL THEORY AND METHOD

Alexander, Jeffrey C. 1982. *Positivism, Presuppositions, and Current Controversies*. Berkeley and Los Angeles: University of California Press.

————. 1984. "Social-Structural Analysis: Some Notes on Its History and Prospects." *The Sociological Quarterly* 25:5–26.

————. 1988. *Action and Its Environments: Toward a New Synthesis*. New York: Columbia University Press.

————. 1990. "Beyond the Epistemological Dilemma: General Theory in a Postpositivist Mode." *Sociological Forum* 5:531–544.

Amato, Joseph A. 1990. *Victims and Values: A History and a Theory of Suffering*. New York: Greenwood Press.

Archer, Margaret S. 1988. *Culture and Agency: The Place of Culture in Social Theory*. Cambridge: Cambridge University Press.

Bernstein, Richard J. 1971. *Praxis and Action: Contemporary Philosophies of Human Activity*. Philadelphia: University of Pennsylvania Press.

Blauner, Bob. 1987. "Problems of Editing 'First-Person' Sociology." *Qualitative Sociology* 10:46–64.

Blumer, Herbert. 1969. *Symbolic Interactionism: Perspective and Method.* Englewood Cliffs, N.J.: Prentice-Hall.

Bourdieu, Pierre. 1977. *Outline of a Theory of Practice.* London: Cambridge University Press.

Brewer, William F. 1986. "What Is Autobiographical Memory?" Pp. 25–49 in D. Rubin (ed.), *Autobiographical Memory.* Cambridge: Cambridge University Press.

Charon, Joel M. 1992. *Symbolic Interactionism: An Introduction, an Interpretation, an Integration.* 4th ed. Englewood Cliffs, N.J.: Prentice-Hall.

Coles, Robert. 1975. "The Method." Pp. 165–181 in R. Lifton (ed.), *Explorations in Psychohistory.* New York: Simon and Schuster.

Collins, Randall. 1981. "On the Microfoundations of Macrosociology." *American Journal of Sociology* 86:984–1014.

Denzin, Norman K. 1970. *The Research Act in Sociology: A Theoretical Introduction to Sociological Methods.* Chicago: Aldine.

———. 1989a. *Interpreting Biography.* Newbury Park, Calif.: Sage.

———. 1989b. *Interpretive Interactionism.* Newbury Park, Calif.: Sage.

———. 1989c. *The Research Act in Sociology: A Theoretical Introduction to Sociological Methods.* 3rd ed. Englewood Cliffs, N.J.: Prentice-Hall.

———. 1991a. *Images of the Postmodern.* Newbury Park, Calif.: Sage.

———. 1991b. "Representing Lived Experiences in Ethnographic Texts." Pp. 59–70 in N. Denzin (ed.), *Studies in Symbolic Interaction.* Vol. 12. Greenwich, Conn.: JAI Press.

Detmer, David. 1988. *Freedom as a Value: A Critique of the Ethical Theory of Jean-Paul Sartre.* La Salle, Ill.: Open Court.

Dworkin, Andrea. 1979. *Pornography: Men Possessing Women.* New York: Perigee.

Fine, Gary Alan. 1991. "On the Macrofoundations of Microsociology: Constraint and the Exterior Reality of Structure." *The Sociological Quarterly* 32:161–177.

Firestone, Shulamith. 1970. *The Dialectic of Sex.* New York: William Morrow.

Giddens, Anthony. 1976. *New Rules of Sociological Method: A Positive Critique of Interpretative Sociologies.* New York: Basic Books.

———. 1979. *Central Problems in Social Theory: Action, Structure and Contradiction in Social Analysis.* Berkeley and Los Angeles: University of California Press.

———. 1984. *The Constitution of Society: Outline of the Theory of Structuration.* Berkeley and Los Angeles: University of California Press.

Glaser, Barney G., and Anselm L. Strauss. 1964. "Awareness Contexts and Social Interaction." *American Sociological Review* 29:669–679.

———. 1967. *The Discovery of Grounded Theory.* Chicago: Aldine.

———. 1971. *Status Passages.* Chicago: Aldine Atherton.

Goffman, Erving. 1959. *The Presentation of Self in Everyday Life.* Garden City, N.Y.: Doubleday.

————. 1961. *Asylums: Essays on the Social Situation of Mental Patients and Other Inmates.* Garden City, N.Y.: Anchor.

Gottdiener, M. 1993. "Ideology, Foundationalism, and Sociological Theory." *The Sociological Quarterly* 34:653–671.

Habermas, Jürgen. 1987. *The Theory of Communicative Action.* Vol. 2, *Lifeworld and System: A Critique of Functionalist Reason.* Boston: Beacon Press.

Halbachs, Maurice. 1980. *The Collective Memory.* New York: Harper and Row.

————. 1992. *On Collective Memory.* Edited by L. Coser. Chicago: University of Chicago Press.

Handler, Joel F. 1992. "Postmodernism, Protest, and the New Social Movements." *Law and Society Review* 26:697–731.

Harvey, David. 1989. *The Condition of Postmodernity: An Enquiry into the Origins of Cultural Change.* Cambridge, Mass.: Blackwell.

Helling, Ingeborg K. 1988. "The Life History Method: A Survey and a Discussion with Norman K. Denzin." Pp. 211–243 in N. Denzin (ed.), *Studies in Symbolic Interaction.* Vol. 9. Greenwich, Conn: JAI Press.

Johnson, John M., and David L. Altheide. 1991. "Text Without Context and the Problem of Authority in Ethnographic Research." Pp. 53–57 in N. Denzin (ed.), *Studies in Symbolic Interaction.* Vol. 12. Greenwich, Conn.: JAI Press.

Kaminer, Wendy. 1993. *I'm Dysfunctional, You're Dysfunctional: The Recovery Movement and Other Self-Help Fashions.* New York: Vintage.

Katovich, Michael A., and Charles MacMurray. 1991. "Toward a Postmodern Theory of the Past." Pp. 73–88 in N. Denzin (ed.), *Studies in Symbolic Interaction.* Vol. 12. Greenwich, Conn.: JAI Press.

Mills, C. Wright. 1959. *The Sociological Imagination.* New York: Oxford University Press.

Musolf, Gil Richard. 1993. "Some Recent Directions in Symbolic Interactionism." Pp. 231–263 in L. Reynolds, *Interactionism: Exposition and Critique.* 3rd ed. Dix Hills, N.Y.: General Hall.

Reynolds, Larry T. 1993. *Interactionism: Exposition and Critique.* 3rd ed. Dix Hills, N.Y.: General Hall.

Ritzer, George. 1992. *Contemporary Sociological Theory.* 3rd ed. New York: McGraw-Hill.

Robinson, John A. 1986. "Temporal Reference Systems and Autobiographical Memory." Pp. 159–188 in D. Rubin (ed.), *Autobiographical Memory.* Cambridge: Cambridge University Press.

Rosenau, Pauline Marie. 1992. *Post-Modernism and the Social Sciences: Insights, Inroads, and Intrusions.* Princeton, N.J.: Princeton University Press.

Rosenwald, George C., and Richard L. Ochberg (eds.). 1992. *Storied Lives: The Cultural Politics of Self-Understanding.* New Haven, Conn.: Yale University Press.

Ryan, William. 1971. *Blaming the Victim.* New York: Vintage.

Sartre, Jean-Paul. 1956. *Being and Nothingness.* Translated by H. Barnes. Secaucus, N.J.: Citadel Press.

Schuman, Howard, and Jacqueline Scott. 1989. "Generations and Collective Memories." *American Sociological Review* 54:359–381.

Schwartz, Barry. 1991. "Iconography and Collective Memory: Lincoln's Image in the American Mind." *The Sociological Quarterly* 32:301–319.

Sewell, William H. Jr. 1992. "A Theory of Structure: Duality, Agency, and Transformation." *American Journal of Sociology* 98:1–29.

Sykes, Charles J. 1992. *A Nation of Victims: The Decay of the American Character.* New York: St. Martin's Press.

Thompson, Paul. 1978. *The Voice of the Past: Oral History.* New York: Oxford University Press.

Turner, Victor M. 1986. "Dewey, Dilthey, and Drama: An Essay on the Anthropology of Experience." Pp. 33–44 in V. Turner and E. Bruner (eds.), *The Anthropology of Experience.* Urbana: University of Illinois Press.

Wright, Susan. 1993. "Blaming the Victim, Blaming Society, or Blaming the Discipline: Fixing Responsibility for Homelessness." *The Sociological Quarterly* 34:1–16.

Index

LIVERPOOL
JOHN MOORES UNIVERSITY
TRUEMAN STREET LIBRARY
TEL. 051 231 4022/4023